TRELOWETH'S

**Treloweth Primary School's collection of recipes
from
lots of people who enjoy cooking!**

The Hypatia Trust

First published in 1999
by The Hypatia Trust

Printed in Great Britain

Printed and bound by
Troutbeck Press, a subsidiary of R Booth (Bookbinder) Ltd
Antron Hill, Mabe, Penryn, Cornwall

Cover design
Bob Derbyshire of RD Design Associates, Truro, Cornwall

Cover drawing by Jody Long
Treloweth School

ISBN   1   872229 37   9

From Phillip Schofield

I am really thrilled to be writing the foreword to your recipe book, as well as being able to contribute a recipe of my own.

So many of the recipes in your book sound really mouth-watering. Prince Charles' Basil and Pine Kernel Bread, Wallace and Gromit's Cheese, Leek and Onion Puffs and Dawn French's Chocolate Fruit Fondue just ask to be made and enjoyed. There are more than 100 tempting recipes to choose from and the list of contributors is amazing.

Your Cornish recipes are all reminders of home. I grew up in Cornwall, and some of them really remind me of happy days gone by. There's nothing like a good home-made pasty or a proper cream tea with splits, jam and clotted cream!

I'm sure that Treloweth School's recipe book is going to be a real favourite with everybody who sees and buys it. It's bound to sell really well for you, and help to raise lots of money for your school funds!

With my very best wishes & good luck to everybody at Treloweth Primary School

from

Phillip Schofield

TRELOWETH SCHOOL

Higher Broadlane, Redruth, Cornwall TR15 3JL   01209 216192

We are very proud and delighted to present our School's very first recipe book. The idea had very simple beginnings, but since then it has grown and grown into the exciting book you now hold. We've been overwhelmed by the tremendous level of response, and everyone's kindness and interest in our project.

We are especially grateful for the help and support given by Prince Charles with the recipe from his Executive Chef at Highgrove House. We understand that the Royal Family very rarely does this!

This recipe book would not have been possible without the hard work of one of our Governors, Keith Thompson and his wife Susie. They have been responsible for making all the phone calls, writing all the letters, typing all the recipes and compiling this book over the past nine months.

I know that you will be delighted by the pictures in our book, which were nearly all drawn by children from Treloweth School.

A very special 'thank you' must also go to Teresa Mazzeo and Bob Derbyshire. Teresa contacted all our sponsors, who gave financial backing for our book. Bob, of RD Design Associates in Truro, helped us with advice and our book's cover design.

You'll find that there's a recipe for just about everyone. I'm sure that you'll have as much fun and pleasure reading and making some of the recipes, as we've had collecting and trying them ourselves!

Bon Appétit!

Karen Budenshire
HEADTEACHER.

CONTENTS

FROM PRINCE CHARLES

BASIL AND PINE KERNEL BREAD

His Royal Highness has kindly agreed to contribute a recipe. Basil and Pine Kernel Bread is one of the breads that we bake regularly at Highgrove, and I hope that it will be enjoyed by all those who purchase your book.

1 lb strong white flour	1½ oz fresh yeast
1 lb strong wholemeal flour	1 tsp Muscavado sugar
1 tsp salt	½ pt tepid water
2 oz sesame seeds	½ pt tepid milk
4 oz toasted pine kernels	4 tbsp malt extract
2 tbsp olive oil	1 bunch fresh basil

Combine flours, salt, sesame seeds, pine kernels and olive oil in a large bowl and mix.

Mix yeast with sugar and 4 tablespoons of tepid water – leave to stand in a warm place for 10 mins to froth. Combine milk and malt extract and warm gently (may appear to curdle slightly – don't worry!)

Gradually mix warm liquids into dry ingredients – ideally in a heavy duty Kenwood, alternatively by hand. Add basil leaves – either whole or shredded. Knead well for approx 10 minutes until dough reshapes itself when compressed. (It is very important that the dough is slightly moist at this stage, as it will absorb more moisture during proving.)

Leave in a warm place – covered – to prove for 10-15 mins until dough has almost doubled in size. Knock back – and shape into desired form – loaves, baguettes or rolls. Preheat oven to Gas Mark 8/230°C/450°F.

Place in oiled loaf tins or onto an oiled baking tray. Leave to rise for 10 mins. Cook loaves for approx 30 mins. Baguettes 15-18 mins. Rolls 12 mins. To test, tap bottom of loaf and it should sound hollow.

When cooked rub crust with melted butter – leave to cool on a rack – wrapped in a tea towel if you prefer a softer less "crusty" loaf.

Carolyn Robb
Executive Chef to HRH The Prince of Wales.

SOUPS AND STARTERS

CHICKEN LIVER PÂTÉ

2 pots of frozen chicken livers
6 oz butter
1 large onion
Cream
Brandy (optional)
Raw vegetables (optional)

Allow the chicken livers to completely defrost (ideally overnight).

Chop the large onion and keep some in reserve for later. Melt together approximately 4oz of butter and add the livers and most of the onion. Mix well together. Cook slowly until there is no red left in the livers.

Remove from the heat and blend with the raw onion and any other raw vegetables you want to add, such as celery, pepper, mushrooms, etc. Add cream, a little salt, black pepper and brandy and mix well. Put mixture into a dish (or two smaller dishes). Melt the remaining butter and pour over the top of the pâté. Leave in the fridge to set (several hours).

Serve as a starter or snack with a little salad and warm toast.

Options: Instead of brandy you could use red wine. When adding the cream, you could add some whole peppercorns.

Barbara Windsor

BEETROOT BORSCHT SOUP

6 medium size beetroot
1 small onion, if liked, chopped finely
Cup of vegetable stock or water
2 lemons
White or light brown sugar
Small carton soured cream or natural yoghurt
Black pepper and salt
2 bay leaves
4 medium size potatoes, peeled (optional, see below)

Cook the beetroot in plenty of boiling, salted water for an hour. Test carefully with a skewer, and if they are not soft, cook for an extra 20-30 minutes on a lower heat. Drain and leave to cool. Carefully remove the skins from the beetroot, which should be soft enough to slice. (If you are using the chopped onion, cook it at the same time as you cook the beetroot.) Put the beetroot (and the optional onion) into a blender with the cup of stock or water. Blend until smooth – it won't be very thick as you put it back into a clean saucepan. Reheat, add the bay leaves and simmer for half an hour.

Now comes the personal touch. As the soup simmers, gradually add the juice of one lemon and 2 tablespoons of sugar. Stir and taste. The aim is to achieve a pleasant sweet-sour flavour. You may need the juice of the second lemon and some more sugar before you are finally satisfied. This is very personal. Season with salt and pepper to taste. Remove the bay leaves. When ready, pour into bowls and add a dob of cream or yoghurt which, as released, gives a pleasant reminder of raspberries and cream.

If the soup is served in summer, it should be slightly chilled with a sprig of mint to garnish. If served in winter, it should be hot and the addition of a boiled potato to each bowl is most pleasant. This is a favourite soup in Jewish homes and restaurants and is often drunk cool in glasses. I have had Borscht both ways. Enjoy!

Rosemary Squires

3

SCOTTISH VEGETABLE BROTH

8 oz dry mixed pulses (marrowfat peas, lentils, pearl barley,
  haricot beans) soaked for 2 hours
1 leek
3 sticks celery
2 medium sized potatoes
1 small swede
3 large carrots (one diced and two grated)
1½ pints stock (can be made with vegetable cubes for vegetarians
  or flank mutton/stewing beef for meat eaters)
6 pints boiling water
Salt and pepper
Fresh parsley

Bring stock and water to the boil in a large (8 pint capacity) pan. Add mixed pulses, and bring back to the boil and simmer for approx 45 minutes. Chop vegetables and grate carrots – add to broth. Season to taste. Simmer for 1 hour.

Add freshly chopped parsley to individual bowls of broth and serve with fresh crusty bread.

Craig Rich
BBC Spotlight South West

LEEK AND POTATO SOUP

2 tbsp olive oil   *500 g potatoes (diced)*
1 onion (chopped)   *500 g leeks (sliced)*
1 clove of garlic (chopped) *750 ml chicken or vegetable stock*
Chopped parsley to garnish

Heat the oil in a large saucepan. Add the onion and garlic, and fry gently for 4-5 minutes. Add the potatoes and leeks and coat well in the oil. Add the stock and bring to the boil. Simmer for 15-20 minutes until vegetables are tender. Liquidize in a food processor or blender. Pour into serving bowls and garnish with parsley. Serve with plenty of crusty bread. A delicious recipe from –

David Blunkett MP
Secretary of State
for Education and Employment

GOAT IN THE THROAT
CREAMY GRILLED MUSHROOMS

You will need for one starter size portion

50 g nanny Cheddar, grated
10 fresh basil leaves, plus small sprigs for garnish
5 or 6 mushrooms wiped clean with a paper towel
100 ml whipping cream
100 g soft butter
1 tbsp chopped parsley
Tube of garlic purée

Add a teaspoonful of the garlic purée, or as much as you can stand, to the butter, together with two thirds of the chopped parsley. Mix well together, using a clean hand to give it a good squidge. Your fingers smell of garlic for ages afterwards – lovely!

Then spread some butter on the bottom of each mushroom and place them stalk upwards on a metal plate or shallow oven-proof dish. Tear – don't chop – the basil leaves onto the mushrooms and put the grated cheese on top of that. Now drizzle the cream over all that. Place under a pre-heated grill until it all goes brown and bubbly and the sauce thickens. Alternatively bake in a hot oven for 8 to 10 minutes. Garnish with the sprigs of basil and the remaining parsley. Serve with crusty French bread. Scrummy.

You can use any left over garlic butter spread onto a French stick cut in half lengthways. Sprinkle with sesame, black onion or fennel seeds. Grill until light brown. Even more scrummy.

Steve Whittingham
Fodders Restaurant, Truro

WESTCOUNTRY'S WINTER WARMER
CURRIED PARSNIP SOUP

2 lb parsnips (peeled and cut into rough chunks)
1 large onion, chopped
1 tsp mild curry powder
3 pints chicken stock
½ pint single cream
Knob of butter

Soften the onion with the butter in a large saucepan. Add the parsnips and stir for another five minutes. Add the curry powder and allow to cook for a further three minutes. Then add the stock, bring to the boil, cover with a lid and simmer for twenty minutes. Remove from the heat and check the parsnips are soft. Put through the liquidizer and then return to the saucepan. Stir in the cream, bring back to the boil and serve immediately with hot crusty bread in front of the telly!

Sarah Lillicrap
Westcountry Television

SMOKED MACKEREL PÂTÉ

Use soft cheese and smoked mackerel to make a creamy pâté with a deliciously smoky flavour. This is simple to prepare and is perfect with fresh warm toast.

220 g pack skinned smoked mackerel
125 g low fat soft cheese
5 ml lemon juice
Freshly ground black pepper
Half lemon wedges to garnish – optional
Toast to serve

Check that the mackerel is free from bones. Put mackerel, cheese, lemon juice and plenty of pepper into a food processor and blend until smooth. (Or you can mash all the ingredients together in a bowl with a fork until fairly smooth.) Transfer the mixture to four small dishes and level the surface of each. Chill in the refrigerator until required. Garnish each dish with lemon wedges and serve with fresh warm toast. Serves 4.

Glynis Bunt
School Governor

MUSHROOM SOUP

1 oz butter
Half onion, finely chopped
About 1lb mushrooms, finely chopped
1 - 2 tbsp plain flour
¾ pint chicken stock (or chicken stock cube in water)
½ pint milk (UHT semi-skimmed gives best results)
Salt and pepper to taste

Melt butter in large saucepan. Add onion and sauté for approximately 5 minutes. Add mushrooms and cook until tender. Add about 1 tablespoon of flour (or enough to make a stiffish mixture). Cook for a minute or two. Add stock and milk, mix thoroughly and simmer for 15 – 20 minutes, preferably in a slow oven or cooker. Allow to cool slightly, put in blender, add salt and pepper according to taste and serve.

N.B. This basic recipe can be used for any vegetable soup, e.g. carrot, parsnip (add some curry powder), tomato, watercress, celery, lentil.

Jonathan Harris
Secretary for Education
Cornwall County Council

CREAM CHEESE AND CASHEW NUT PÂTÉ

1 carrot
225 g cream cheese
100 g broken cashew nuts, roasted and ground
1 tbsp chopped parsley
Salt and pepper to taste
Parsley to garnish

Finely grate carrot. Beat all the ingredients together. Press the mixture into individual ramekin dishes and refrigerate until required. Garnish with parsley sprigs and slices of raw carrot. Serve with toast. This can also be used as a sandwich filling.

Frieda Nicholls
School Special Needs Co-ordinator

CREAM CHEESE AND HERB PÂTÉ

Lovely on hot toast, with savoury biscuits, in smoked salmon rolls or with fruit.

5 oz or 150 g butter
1 lb or 450 g cream cheese
Black pepper
2 tbsp mixed chopped herbs
(If you use freeze dried herbs, add them to the melted butter.)

1 clove of garlic
1 tbsp olive oil

1 tbsp chopped parsley

Melt the butter in a small saucepan set over a low heat, pour into a jug and leave to cool. Unwrap and place the cheese in a large mixing bowl, add the oil and herbs. Peel the garlic clove and crush it over the assembled ingredients.

Rest the bowl on a damp tea towel and using a wooden spoon, vigorously beat the mixture together until you have a smooth texture. Gradually blend in the cool butter, taste, twist in black pepper and taste again. Cover the surface with clingfilm and chill for about an hour.

Ann Long
Master Chef of Great Britain
The Bassett Count House, Carnkie

CULLEN SKINK

Skink comes from the Gaelic and originally meant 'essence'. Nowadays it usually means a stew-soup or chowder type dish. This recipe is traditional to the shores of the Moray Firth and is delicious. Serves 4.

1 smoked haddock (preferably Finnan)
Water
1 chopped onion
1 pint milk
Hot mashed potato, quantity varies, depending on the thickness of soup you want
1 - 2 oz butter
Chopped parsley (optional)
Salt and pepper

Skin the haddock and put in a shallow pan with just enough cold water to cover. Bring to the boil and add the chopped onion. Simmer until cooked – about 5 to 10 minutes. Lift the fish from the pan and remove the bones. Put the bones back into the pan with the fish stock and onions and cook for another half-hour.

Meanwhile prepare the potatoes. Mash them whilst hot, adding a little butter. Flake the fish and put to one side. Strain the fish bone stock carefully into a clean pan. Add the slightly warmed milk, the flaked fish and enough hot mashed potato to give a creamy consistency. Stir in the butter and season to taste. Serve very hot. Garnish with the chopped parsley, if you like it.

Anne Webb
Teacher, Class 6

KATHLEEN'S CAULIFLOWER SOUP

1 fully grown cauliflower
2 oz butter
Seasoning (that's salt, pepper, etc)
Grated cheese

¾ pint chicken stock
1 oz plain flour

The cauliflower should be mature, not too hefty and a medium size will do. Simmer the said vegetable in enough water, leaving on all the stalk and the crisp green outer leaves. When cooked (this is up to you to judge, could be a mere 3 minutes with a garden-fresh specimen, but a lot longer with a more elderly plant) liquidize it.

Then melt the butter in a pan and stir in the flour to make a roux. (A roux is what you get when you stir melted butter with flour.) Stir in a generous quantity of grated cheese. Add the chicken stock gradually and bring the whole shooting match to the boil. Now add the liquid cauliflower and cook for just a few minutes more. This never goes wrong when Kathleen does it, and has a good chance of working well when others do it.

Some connoisseurs like to add more grated cheese or even double cream (a dash) to the finished creation. Sling in the seasoning at more or less any stage, as you feel fit. This one will run and run.

Sir Tim Rice

9

FISH

BANKER'S FISH PIE

1 lb fish, two thirds cod and one third smoked haddock
1 salmon steak   4 oz peeled prawns
2 hardboiled eggs   1 - 1½ lb mashed potato
2 tbsp plain flour   2½ oz butter
½ pint milk   4 oz grated cheese
Scallops (optional)

Gently poach fish until cooked. Peel the skin and flake the flesh. Place in an ovenproof dish and sprinkle with chopped hardboiled eggs and prawns. Make a white sauce and add two ounces of the grated cheese. A little white wine and some scallops can be added if desired. Pour the sauce over the fish, then spread the mashed potato on top and decorate the top with the back of a fork. Sprinkle with the rest of the grated cheese and heat through in oven at 180°C. This freezes well. Put under the grill to brown the cheese before serving.

Eddie George, Governor of The Bank of England

RICHARD'S TUNA CASSEROLE

1 medium tin mushroom soup
1 medium tin tuna, drained
1 small tin of sweetcorn, drained, or one small packet of frozen
½ tsp dried herbs
4 oz button mushrooms halved
2 oz shelled prawns
1 bayleaf
1 small glass white wine (optional)
Freshly ground black pepper to taste.
2 packets salted crisps (crushed)
2 packets salted crisps (uncrushed)

Mix everything in an ovenproof dish, saving the two packets of uncrushed crisps for the topping. Sprinkle the uncrushed crisps in a layer over the top. Bake in a medium hot oven for about 20 minutes.

**Richard Madeley and Judy Finnegan
ITV's This Morning**

EMETT'S SEAFOOD PASTA

1 lb seafood cocktail
Oil or butter
Large onion
Clove garlic
Large tin chopped tomatoes with herbs or a teaspoon of mixed herbs
Salt and pepper to taste

Chop onion and fry in butter or oil with garlic until onion is soft but not brown. Add seafood cocktail and tomatoes and allow to simmer for 10 minutes. Add seasoning to taste. Serve with spaghetti or tagliatelle. To make this dish spicy you can add either Tabasco or chilli powder.

This is one of Emett and Liz's favourites. Liz in particular likes it because, unlike her coffee mornings with Hyacinth, most of the pasta stays on the plate – not on the floor!

NOTE:
On no account must this dish be served on Royal Doulton with the Blue Periwinkles. I use lots of garlic and chilli. Hyacinth won't come anywhere near me !!

David Griffin
Emett in "Keeping Up Appearances"

TARTE AUX MOULES

For the pastry:
8 oz plain flour   2½ oz chilled butter
2½ oz chilled lard   1½ - 2 tbsp water
1 egg white   ½ tsp salt

Pre-heat the oven to 200°C/400°F/Gas Mark 6.

Sift the flour and salt into a food processor or a mixing bowl, add the chilled butter and lard cut into pieces. Work together until the mixture looks like fine breadcrumbs. Stir in the water with a table knife until it comes together into a ball. Turn out on to a lightly floured surface and knead briefly until smooth. Roll out and use to line a 25cm/10 inch loose-bottomed tin, 4cm/1½ inches deep. Prick the base here and there with a fork and chill for 20 minutes.

Line the pastry case with a sheet of crumpled greaseproof paper, fill with baking beans and bake blind for 15 minutes. Remove the paper and beans and return the pastry to the oven for 5 minutes. Remove once more and brush the base with the unbeaten egg white. Return to the oven for 1 minute, remove and lower the oven temperature to 190°C/375°F/Gas Mark 5.

For the filling:
2 lb mussels, cleaned   2 fl oz dry white wine
3 tbsp chopped parsley (keep the stalks)   5-6 shallots finely chopped
1 oz butter   3 eggs, beaten
5 garlic cloves finely chopped   10 fl oz double cream
Salt and freshly ground black pepper

Put the mussels into a large pan with the wine and parsley stalks. Cover and cook over a high heat for 3-4 minutes, shaking the pan every now and then, until the mussels have opened. Tip them into a colander set over a bowl to collect all the cooking liquor. Leave to cool slightly and then remove the mussels from their shells, discarding any that have not opened.

Melt the butter in a pan, add the shallots and garlic and cook gently for about 7 minutes, until very soft. Add all but the last tablespoon or two of the mussel cooking liquor and simmer rapidly until it has evaporated. Scrape the mixture into a bowl and leave to cool. Then stir in the eggs, cream and parsley and season to taste with pepper and a little salt if necessary.

Scatter the mussels over the base of the pastry case and pour in the egg mixture. Bake for 25-30 minutes, until just set and lightly browned. Remove and leave to cool slightly before serving.
Serve with a green salad. Serves 8 people.

**Rick Stein
The Seafood Restaurant, Padstow**

ITALIAN STALLION SALMON

*A pack of fresh tagliatelle
¼ to ½ lb smoked salmon pieces
½ pint single cream
Lump of fresh Parmesan cheese
Fresh ground pepper*

Put water on to boil. Add pasta and cook according to instructions.

In a separate pan gently heat the cream. Add the grated cheese and gently melt. Add the salmon pieces. When the pasta is ready, cool it down a little and drain it off. Add it to the sauce and stir.

Serve in heated bowls and add black pepper to taste. Enjoy.

**Mark Foreman
Book Illustrator**

TROUT IN OATMEAL

Gut and clean trout. Make a batter using 1 cup of oatmeal and 2 beaten eggs. Add pepper and salt for seasoning and mix together. Paint or dip fish in the batter.

Grill or fry for approximately 10 to 15 minutes, using medium heat until golden brown, adding some extra coating to the top while cooking.

Dress with watercress and serve with baby tomatoes and new potatoes. Serve with a fresh white wine. Enjoy.

Roger Daltrey

PASTA WITH TOMATO AND TUNA

Serves 3 rugby players or 6 Treloweth School Children!

1 medium onion, chopped
1 celery stick, chopped
1 red pepper, chopped
1 garlic clove, crushed
150 ml/¼ pint chicken stock
400 g canned chopped tomatoes
30 ml/2 tbsp capers in vinegar, drained
Salt and pepper

10 ml/1 tsp castor sugar
15 ml/1 tbsp chopped basil
15 ml/1 tbsp chopped parsley
450 g pasta shells
400 g canned tuna in brine, drained
15ml/1 tbsp tomato purée

Put chopped onion, celery, red pepper and garlic into a pan. Add the stock, bring to the boil and cook for 5 minutes or until the stock has almost completely gone. Add the tomatoes, tomato purée, sugar and herbs. Season to taste and bring to the boil. Simmer for 30 minutes until thick, stir occasionally.

Meanwhile cook the pasta in boiling water, drain thoroughly and transfer into a warm serving dish. Flake the tuna into large chunks and add to the sauce with the capers. Heat gently for 1-2 minutes, pour over the pasta, toss gently and serve immediately.

Rob Thirlby
Saracens Rugby Football Club

NAT'S TUNA PASTA

1 tin tuna
2 handfuls pasta shells
1 handful sweetcorn
Low calorie salad cream

Cook pasta in pan. Mix tuna with salad cream in a bowl. Add sweetcorn to pasta, when it is cooked and drained. Add the tuna mix and more salad cream. Very simple because I can't cook!!

Natalie Cornah
BBC Spotlight South West

LINGUINE AI GAMBERI

Long, thin pasta
5 oz butter
12-16 oz fresh prawns
1 tbsp Madras curry powder
6 tbsp dry white wine (more if liked)
½ pint chicken stock
10 oz grated Parmesan cheese
Salt and ground black pepper
4 tbsp chopped mint
2 egg yolks and 1 whole egg

Start pasta cooking. Heat half butter in a large pan, add prawns and Madras curry powder. Cook for 2 minutes. Add wine and stir well, then add the stock. Mix the eggs and Parmesan in a bowl.

When the pasta is 'al dente', drain and put into pan with prawns. Add remaining butter and egg and Parmesan mixture. Mix together well. Add salt and black pepper to taste. Finally add the mint and serve.

Ken Abbott
Teacher Class 8

TUNA AND MACARONI SALAD

A recipe for healthy eating and building up your strength!

Combine half a pound of cooked fresh or dried macaroni while still warm with a tin of tuna in brine, a bunch of washed and chopped spring onions, a few chopped small sticks of celery, a chopped red pepper and salt and black pepper to taste.

Then add several tablespoons of your favourite salad dressing along with lots of chopped parsley and any other herbs you fancy. Turn onto a bed of green salad and decorate with tomato slices. Should serve at least four.

David Beckham
Manchester United FC

PRAWN AND COURGETTE CURRY

350 g frozen prawns, de-frosted and patted dry with a paper kitchen towel
350 g courgettes, cut to prawn size
6 cloves garlic, finely chopped
1 green chilli, chopped
1 tsp grated fresh ginger
½ tsp turmeric
1 heaped tsp ground cumin
¼ tsp cayenne
30 g fresh coriander or parsley, finely chopped
1 tin tomatoes, chopped with a little of the juice
1 tbsp lemon juice
Salt
Vegetable oil

Sprinkle courgettes with salt. Leave for 30 minutes, then drain and pat dry. Fry the garlic in a little vegetable oil until golden. Add all the other ingredients except for the prawns, bring to simmer for 5 minutes. Then add the prawns and simmer for another 3 minutes.

This is great with RAITA

1 small carton natural yoghurt
4 cm length cucumber, grated
1 small bunch of fresh mint, finely chopped
½ tsp ground cumin
Cayenne pepper- maximum of ¼ tsp

Mix all the ingredients together and serve cold with the hot Prawn and Courgette Curry.

Mike Jelbert
Teacher, Class 7

'TIME TEAM' SALMON IN SALT DOUGH

One of the activities in every episode of Time Team is when an old craft is demonstrated. You can't get a much older craft than cooking, so when we went to a deserted medieval village on the banks of the Tyne we decided to try out a recipe from the 13th-15th centuries. We are lucky that many of the recipes were written down in manuscripts of the period and here's one you might like to experiment with.

First catch your fish! This would have been easy in medieval times, but the Tyne is not much of a salmon river nowadays. Despite having made a pretty good trap out of willow and hazel baskets with an ingenious trap at one end to catch the fish, we stood half dressed in a freezing northern river in November with no results. So a quick trip to the nearest fishmongers was needed!

This method is good for any fish. Gut the fish and stuff it. For the stuffing use fresh breadcrumbs, herbs, dried fruit, seasoning, butter and a bit of stock. How much you will need depends on what size fish you have. You can use fine sticks through the skin to hold it in or even sew it up. Then cover it in the dough. Make this simply by mixing flour and water together with a lot of salt. Not too wet, not too dry. A bread dough consistency is good. How much? Once again it depends on the size of the fish. You need enough to wrap the entire fish like a Cornish pasty, with a covering of at least half an inch of dough.

Then cook it in the embers of a fire. You need to cover the whole parcel with hot ash and glowing coals. Don't bother with burning wood as this will burn the outside and leave the middle raw, which won't do at all. For a full sized salmon well covered in dough and buried in plenty of hot embers, we usually allow at least 1¼ hours to ensure it's done. The moisture in the fish is trapped by the dough, so your salmon, bream, whiting, whatever is lovely and tender. The salt will add to the flavour and, as Tony Robinson remarked, it will be one of the best things you have tasted. Be very careful when using the fire (you can use an oven of course, but the wood smoke does add to the flavour) and use a spade and gloves when putting it in and out.

Enjoy the fish and give the remains of the crust to the dogs or peasants gathered around your table! If you like you could also make a sauce to go with it – puréed green herbs with sharp white wine would be good, or try mixing some apricot jam, red wine, ginger and almonds (a common medieval sauce thickener) for something a little different.

Written by Mark Griffin, fish caught by Bodger Hodgeson, cooked by Madeleine Hodgeson, eaten by the Time Team Cast and Crew.

MEAT

CHUN-PI CHICKEN

My favourite recipe is Chun-Pi Chicken, which is hot and spicy and comes from the Szechuan region of China. If you don't like chilli reduce the amount of chilli you add. You don't have to eat the whole spices; they are there for flavour.

4 chicken breasts
3 tbsp soya sauce
1½ tbsp sherry
2 tsp salt
5 star anise (whole from Chinese shop)
10 dried chillies (less if you prefer)
2 tbsp dried orange peel (available from Chinese shop,
                    this is called Chun Pi)
½ tbsp Szechuan peppercorns (again from Chinese shop)
1½ tbsp sugar
1 tbsp rice wine
1 tbsp dark vinegar (the Chinese one does make all the difference)
4 tbsp sesame oil
8 cups peanut oil for frying
3 cups water.

Chop chicken into bite sized pieces. Marinade with 2 tablespoons of soya sauce and a teaspoon of salt for half an hour. Heat oil in wok (a large frying pan will do if large enough and has a lid). Cook the chicken for 4 minutes while stirring all the time. Remove.

In the wok heat 3 tablespoons of sesame oil, add star anise, chillies, orange peel and peppercorns. Stir until brown. Add the three cups of water, chicken meat, 1 teaspoon of salt, 1½ tablespoons of sugar, 1 tablespoon of soya sauce, 1½ tablespoon of sherry and the tablespoon of rice wine.

Cook until dry then add the tablespoon of dark vinegar and a tablespoon of sesame oil, mix well and serve. You can eat this dish cold.

Make the effort to get the right ingredients, which will make all the difference.

Charlie Dimmock
BBC TV's Groundforce

PORK CASSEROLE

1 lb chopped lean pork
1 tbsp cooking oil
Small tin chopped tomatoes
1 pint chicken stock
1 tsp sugar`
Salt and pepper to taste

1 onion
3 sliced carrots
1 tbsp flour
2 bay leaves
½ tsp ground nutmeg

Heat the oil. Fry the onion, add the meat and stir in the tablespoon of flour. Add the stock and bring to the boil. Add the tin of chopped tomatoes and all the other ingredients. Bring back to the boil.

Put in the oven. Cook at 120°C for about one and a half hours, 'til pork is tender. Serve with mashed potatoes and a green vegetable. Serves 4.
My favourite recipe!

Chris Blount
BBC Radio Cornwall

BETTY'S HOTPOT

1½ lb neck of lamb, cubed
1½ lb potatoes, peeled and thinly sliced
1 large or 2 medium onions roughly chopped
¾ pint light stock or hot water
1 tbsp Worcestershire sauce
1 bayleaf
1 tbsp flour
1 oz dripping and 1 oz butter, or 2 oz butter
Salt and pepper to season

Preheat the oven to 170°C/325°F/Gas Mark 5.

Melt the dripping or 1 oz butter over a high heat in a heavy-bottomed frying pan until the fat smokes. Seal the meat and continue frying until nicely browned. Remove the pieces from the pan to a deep casserole or divide among four high-sided, ovenproof dishes.

Turn the heat down to medium. Fry the onions in the pan juices, adding a little more butter or dripping if necessary. When the onions are soft and starting to brown, sprinkle on the flour and stir in to soak up the fat and the juices. As the flour paste starts to colour, start adding stock or water a few tablespoons at a time, stirring vigorously to avoid lumps. Gradually add the rest of the liquid. Bring to a simmer, stirring constantly; add the Worcestershire sauce and season with salt and pepper to taste. Pour the onions and liquid over the meat and mix well. Tuck in the bayleaf (tear into four pieces if making individual hotpots).

Arrange the potatoes over the meat in overlapping layers, seasoning each layer. Dot the top layer of potato with the remainder of the butter. Cover the dish and place on the top shelf of the oven for 2 hours. Uncover and cook for a further 30 minutes. If the potatoes are not brown by this point, turn up the oven and cook for a further 15 minutes, or finish off under the grill, brushing the potato slices with more butter if they look too dry.

From Coronation Street

POT ROAST PHEASANT
WITH PARSNIP, CREAM AND GRAPES

Ideally served with brown Basmati rice and crisp green broccoli. Serves 6.

2 hen pheasants
4 oz cream cheese with garlic
8 oz parsnips
2 oz butter
1 tbsp sunflower oil
2 tsp ground cardamom or mace
¼ pint sweet cider
3 tbsp sherry vinegar
1 heaped tbsp bottled green peppercorns
6 oz green grapes
½ pint double cream
1 tbsp chopped parsley
Sea salt
3-4 pinches cayenne pepper

Loosen the breast skin of pheasants by gently inserting your fingers underneath it. Press the cream cheese under the skin and spread all over the breasts of the birds. Peel the parsnip and cut into small cubes. Melt the butter and oil in a large heatproof casserole over a fairly high heat; add cubes of parsnip and stir round to brown slightly. Add ground cardamom and stir for a minute before adding cider, sherry vinegar, green peppercorns and a sprinkling of sea salt. Remove from heat and place prepared pheasants on top of parsnip mixture.

Preheat oven to Gas Mark 4/350°F/180°C. Cover casserole and cook for 50 minutes, then remove cover and put back for another 10 minutes until pheasants are lightly browned. Remove pheasants from casserole and place on a heated serving plate. Add cream and halved grapes to parsnip and juices. Bring to the boil, bubble for 2 minutes and remove from the heat. Stir in the chopped parsley and pour into sauceboat to serve with pheasants.

Angela Brock
Teacher, Class 2

DAPHNE'S LEMON HONEY CHICKEN

8 chicken breasts   *90 ml (6 tbsp) clear honey*
90 ml (6tbsp) butter   *Juice of 3 lemons*

Pre-heat the oven to 375°F/190°C/Gas Mark 5.

Place the chicken joints in a roasting tin and season with salt and pepper. Melt the honey, butter and lemon juice in a pan over a low heat. Spoon over the chicken. Cook in the pre-heated oven (see above) for 45 minutes or until golden brown. Serves 8. Enjoy!

What I love about this recipe is that it's really easy, tastes stunning and is good enough to serve to friends for supper!

Daphne Skinnard
BBC Radio Cornwall

TURKEY RAGOUT WITH SCONE TOPPING

12 oz diced turkey meat
1 onion, peeled and sliced
8 oz cooking apples
12 oz carrots, peeled and sliced
Salt and pepper
2 level tsp paprika
2 level tsp coriander
½ tsp turmeric
2 level tsp plain flour
1 pint vegetable or chicken stock

Scone topping:
8 oz self-raising flour
1 level tsp baking powder
¼ tsp salt
2 oz margarine
2 tbsp chopped parsley
Milk to mix

Brown the meat in a pan. Add the prepared vegetables and spices. Cook for approximately 5 minutes. Stir in flour and cook for another minute. Gradually add the stock, stirring to mix in the flour. Season and leave to simmer for about 30 minutes. Add more fluid if necessary.

Ten minutes before serving make the scone topping. Rub the margarine into the flour. Add the baking powder, salt and parsley. Mix with the milk to form a dough. Roll out into a thick round. Segment, then cook on a baking sheet at Gas Mark 7 for 10 minutes. Serve the scone on top of the ragout. Serves 4.

Jo Isherwood
School Support Staff

FORMULA 1 MINCE AND TATTIES

This is a recipe which David himself cooked on the programme 'Ready, Steady, Cook' in 1997. This dish reminds David of when he used to live in Scotland. "Good traditional cooking like my mother used to cook."

Lean beef mince
2 potatoes
1 turnip
Beef stock

1 Savoy cabbage
1 onion
2 parsnips
Salt and pepper

Prepare vegetables – peel and dice potatoes, chop onion, slice parsnips, turnips and cabbage. Brown the mince, add a little beef stock, salt and pepper. Add fried onions and cabbage to the mince.

Mash potatoes and pipe a chequered flag onto a serving dish. Spoon the mince into the squares of the flag.

Serve with roast parsnips, buttered cabbage and pickled turnip (marinaded with a little sugar and chilli).

David Coulthard

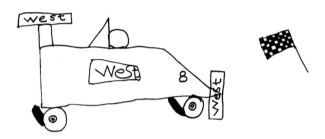

MOCK MOUSSAKA

Here's a recipe for when you can't get your hands on any aubergines, and your friends are arriving in a few hours!! Serves 4.

1 large onion, chopped	*1 lb potatoes, peeled and sliced thinly*
1 lb mince	*1 oz butter*
2 tbsp oil	*1 oz flour*
Pinch mixed herbs	*½ pint milk*
2 tomatoes skinned and chopped	*4 oz grated cheese*
Salt and pepper to taste	

Fry mince and onions in oil for 10 minutes. Add herbs, tomatoes and seasoning. Layer the mince and potatoes in an ovenproof dish. Finish with a layer of potatoes.

Melt butter, add flour and seasoning and cook for 1 minute. Gradually add in the milk, stirring all the time. Stir in half the cheese and pour over mince and potatoes. Sprinkle the remaining cheese on top. Bake for 50 minutes at 190°C. ENJOY!!

Helen Young
BBC Weather Presenter

"GOING BANANAS"

Peel four to six bananas (according to size) and wrap with sliced ham, which has been thinly spread with mild English mustard.

Place the wrapped bananas in an ovenproof dish and cover with a cheese sauce.

Bake in a moderate oven for 20 to 25 minutes, adding some grated cheese on top five minutes before cooking time has finished. Serve hot. Delicious!

Duncan Warren
Pirate FM102 Radio, Redruth

SPECIAL SAUSAGE ROLLS

8 slices of thin-cut ready sliced white bread
100 g/4 oz grated Cheddar cheese (or any other hard cheese you fancy)
50 g/2 oz softened butter or margarine
Salt and pepper
Mustard, or not, to taste
8 pork chipolata sausages
Wooden cocktail sticks

Cut the crusts off the slices of bread. Roll them as flat as you can with a rolling pin. Mix the grated cheese, butter, salt and pepper together very well (and as much mustard as you like), to make a spreading consistency. Divide the mixture between the 8 slices of bread, and spread it evenly over them. Put the sausages on the slices of bread and roll up. Put two cocktail sticks through the uncooked sausage rolls, one at each end. Then cut the rolls in half.

You should have 16 sausage rolls. Put them onto a very lightly greased baking sheet. Pop them into a pre-heated hot oven, 400°F/200°C/Gas Mark 6, for about 25-30 minutes. They should be golden brown and crunchy and make a very tasty hot snack. They are also very good with baked beans or salad.

Jo Frost
Teacher, Class 9

TOAD-IN-THE-HOLE WITH SAGE AND ONIONS

Not an attractive name, admittedly, but it's a delicious classic, especially if you make it with good-quality pork sausages, a little sage and fried onion rings.

1 lb (450 g) pure pork sausages
Beef dripping or lard
2 medium onions, peeled and sliced thinly
6 oz (175 g) plain flour
2 large eggs
6 fl oz (175 ml) milk
4 fl oz (110 ml) water
Salt and freshly milled black pepper
1 level tsp dried sage

Pre-heat the oven to Gas Mark 7/425°F/220°C.

First put a tablespoon of dripping into a solid-based roasting tin (base measuring about 9x7 inch (23x18cm) and pop it into the oven to heat. Then in a frying pan melt some more fat and brown the onions for about 5 minutes or so until they have softened a bit. Remove them to a plate and lightly brown the sausages all round – again for about 5 minutes. While they're browning, make the batter by sifting the flour into a bowl. Make a well in the middle, drop the eggs in and, using an electric hand-whisk (or a fork), whisk the eggs, incorporating the flour and adding the milk and water mixed together first. Season the batter with salt, pepper and sage. When the fat in the tin starts to sizzle, take it out of the oven and keep it sizzling by placing it on top of the stove over a medium heat. Then put in the sausages and the onions on top of them and, making sure that the fat is still very hot, pour in the batter. Quickly shake the tin to get the batter all round the base of the sausages etc., then transfer the tin back to the highest shelf of the oven and let it bake for about 40 minutes or until puffy and crisp. Serve straightaway, with gravy or apple and onion sauce. Serves 4.

Delia Smith

"MERSEY BEAT" SCOUSE   1963 –1999

1 lb lean stewing lamb
1 onion, chopped
2 large carrots, sliced
Approx 3 to 4 large potatoes, peeled and cut into chunky pieces
Salt and pepper
Lamb stock cube and 2 Oxos

Bring meat to boil in large pan and skim. Add potatoes, carrots and onion (leeks and turnips may also be added). Add salt and pepper and crumble in the stock cube and Oxos. Cover and simmer for 1½ - 2 hours.

Adjust flavouring to preferred taste – bay leaves, mixed herbs and tomato purée may be added. The scouse can be left to stand overnight to thicken if preferred.

It tastes brill!!!

Gerry Marsden
Gerry and the Pacemakers

CHICKEN TROPICANA

Ingredients for marinade:

3 tbsp malt vinegar	*½ tsp soy sauce*
2 tsp honey	*Pinch ground ginger*
Juice from 1 x 8 oz can of pineapple rings	
2½ fl oz tomato juice	

4 medium chicken joints (skinned)	*½ oz butter*
1 large carrot cut into strips	*2 level tsp cornflour*
1 x 8 oz can pineapple rings (juice drained for the marinade)	
Salt and pepper to taste	

Place chicken joints in a dish. Mix together the ingredients for the marinade and pour over the chicken. Leave covered for at least 4 hours, turning joints occasionally.

Heat the butter in a frying pan. Remove the chicken joints from the marinade and fry in the butter for about 15 minutes, or until almost cooked. Add carrot strips and pineapple, cut into pieces, and fry for a further two minutes.

Blend the marinade into the cornflour and pour over the chicken. Bring to the boil and simmer for 5 minutes. Serve with rice and vegetables.

Gillian Taylforth
EastEnders

CHEESIE HAMMIE EGGIE

A lunchtime favourite, Cheesie Hammie Eggie is traditional fare throughout the Royal Navy. It is simple to produce and can be served as a snack or a full meal – Naval practice is to add chips and baked beans. Cheesie Hammie Eggie is particularly easy to produce and eat in rough weather!

White sliced bread
Grated Cheddar or other hard cheese
Smoked or plain ham
Egg
Seasoning
Pinch of English mustard and splash of Worcester sauce (both optional)

Lightly toast one side of the bread under a grill and place to one side. Mix the cheese, ham, mustard, Worcester sauce and seasoning together in a blender.

Lightly whisk an egg, and then add enough whisked egg to the blended mixture to form a smooth but not runny, paste. Spread the paste onto the untoasted side of the bread.

Place the bread (paste side up) under a hot grill and heat until the paste has melted. Serve with a fried egg placed on top.

Captain J C Rapp, Royal Navy
HMS Cornwall

KRYTEN'S CREAMY CHICKEN CURRY

The crew of Red Dwarf have trawled through Kryten's database and have come up with one of his Chicken Curry Recipes!

4 oz Basmati rice	*½ tsp ground turmeric*

2 tbsp sunflower oil *1 large onion (8 ozs weight)*
1-2 tbsp garlic purée *1 tsp curry paste*
8 oz boneless, skinless, chicken cut into cubes
4 fl oz chicken stock *14 oz can coconut milk*
1 tbsp mango chutney *½ small lime*
Salt and pepper

½ cucumber *1 plum tomato*
2 spring onions *5 oz carton yoghurt*
1 packet of mini poppadums crisps
Good pinch of paprika

Put the rice into a saucepan with turmeric and ½ pint of boiling salted water. Cover and simmer for about 10 minutes.

Heat sunflower oil in a large frying pan. Thinly slice the onion, and add the garlic purée. Fry over medium heat, until onion is softened. Add chicken to the pan and cook, until just sealed. Add curry paste, and stir-fry for another minute. Pour in the stock, bring to the boil, and boil fast until almost all the liquid has evaporated. Pour in ⅔ of the coconut milk, and season generously with salt and pepper. Stir and simmer for about 6-8 minutes, or until chicken is cooked through and sauce has thickened, adding more coconut milk if necessary.

Cut cucumber into quarters, and remove seeds, and finely chop. Finely chop tomatoes and spring onions. Stir cucumber, tomatoes and spring onions into yoghurt and season to taste with salt and pepper.

Add chutney to the chicken and squeeze in lime juice, cook for a further 1-2 minutes.

Put the rice onto serving plates, and spoon on the chicken mixture. Serve at once with mini poppadums, and cucumber raita, sprinkle with a little paprika.

Kryten
Red Dwarf

Kryten discovers Lister's boxer shorts in the vindaloo

TURKEY NOODLE BAKE

"Noodle bakes are a favourite with American families – warm, comforting, tasty and above all easy to get together. They used to be a popular way to use up left over turkey after Christmas and Thanksgiving but now many people eat turkey throughout the year."

1 onion, chopped
2 fat cloves of garlic, crushed
1 sweet red pepper, cored and sliced
1 stick celery, sliced thinly
2 tbsp olive oil
400 g lean turkey meat – either steaks cut into stir fry strips or mince
250 g tagliatelle or other pasta shapes
125 g mature grated cheese, e.g. Cheddar type or try Gruyere or
Italian Provolone
2-3 tbsp dried breadcrumbs
Sea salt and freshly ground black pepper

Sauce:
25 g butter or sunflower margarine
2 tbsp flour
300 ml milk
300 ml stock
1 tsp dried oregano

Put the pasta on to boil according to pack instructions, then drain and set aside in the colander.

Put the onion, garlic, pepper and celery into a frying pan with the olive oil and heat until it all starts to sizzle. Stir and sauté gently for about 5 minutes until softened. Remove with a slotted spoon. Raise the heat, add the turkey and stir-fry for about 5 minutes then return the vegetables and cook for another 5 minutes.

Put all the sauce ingredients into a saucepan and bring slowly to the boil, stirring briskly with a whisk until it thickens and becomes smooth. Season well and simmer for a minute then mix with the turkey, pasta and two thirds of the cheese. Pour into a baking dish and top with the remaining cheese and the breadcrumbs. Grill the top until golden brown and crispy.
Serve hot. Serves 4.

Loyd Grossman

THE LENNY HENRY KILLER CHILLI

1 lb minced beef
2 green peppers
1 tin kidney beans
2 big onions
1 tin Italian tomatoes
Tomato purée
Chilli powder – mild or not depending on whether your tongue is
made of leather!
Pinch of oregano
Pinch of cloves
Glass of red wine
¼ lb mushrooms
Lucky rabbit's foot!
Pinch of mixed spices
Dash of Tabasco
2 beef Oxo cubes

Place rabbit's foot round your neck (you're going to need all the luck you can get because I certainly don't know what I'm doing)!

Chop onions and green peppers. Fry in about 4oz butter until they are fairly translucent (that means see-through, thicky). Add the meat and fry until it is brown. Add the tomato purée (about 1 tbsp) and stir until sauce thickens. Add all the spices and herbs, chop mushrooms, add them and stir for 2 minutes. Add kidney beans and give it a good stir. Add dash of Tabasco and crumble in Oxo cubes and wine and stir again. Put on a low heat and simmer for about one hour, stirring occasionally. After this time it should be a lovely dark brown colour and quite thick. If there is a layer of fat on top, scrape off with a spoon. Serve with rice or pitta bread to about 4 people.

Yum Yum in my Tum!

Lenny Henry

ZAPPED SPAGHETTI

Any quantity of:
Minced beef
Mushrooms
Tinned tomatoes
Pasta
Bacon
Salt
Tomato purée
Onion/green peppers/garlic if you like them. Freddy says he needs indigestion tablets when he eats these!
Parmesan cheese. Freddy says he thinks that Parmesan cheese smells like old socks, but that doesn't stop you having some on the top, if you like the stuff!

Make the sauce as usual and simmer for as long as possible. Boil the pasta. Mix all together in one saucepan and serve.

Freddy Zapp

SAUSAGE, STUFFING AND BANANA PIE

A real winter warmer, tummy filler and invention of Brian Terry (husband of Liz Terry, headteacher of Pool School).

This is a dish which can be expanded to feed more, or just hungrier, mouths. The ingredients below serve 2 to 4 depending on accompanying vegetables and/or portion size.

1 medium onion
4 good quality large sausages
1 banana
1 stock cube
1 small packet of sage and onion stuffing mix
28 g (1 oz) grated Cheddar cheese
Mashed potato to form topping (depends on size of dish and
personal choice of depth
A little vegetable oil for frying

Finely chop the onions and fry gently until clear and slightly browned. Grill or fry the sausages until light brown and largely cooked. Slice the banana into 3 long strips and put between the sausages arranged at the bottom of an ovenproof dish. Put the fried onions in the gaps between the banana and sausages. Sprinkle a thin layer of stuffing mix over the sausage/banana/onion layer. Make up the stock using hot water and pour a little of this into the bottom of the dish so that it soaks into the stuffing. You can spice it up by adding some Worcestershire Sauce in with the stock if you fancy it. Leave to stand for a few minutes to make sure that you have added enough to stop the stuffing from being too dry. Fork mashed potato over the top and then sprinkle with cheese.

Put into a hot oven, 180°C (sorry but I do not use gas!), for about 40 minutes until the topping is nicely browned. Serve with vegetables of your choice, baked beans or on its own. A real rib sticker, hot and filling for a winter meal.

Liz Terry
Head of Pool School, Redruth

FILETS MIGNONS
WITH MUSHROOMS AND SHALLOTS

100 g chopped shallots
200 g sliced mushrooms
50 ml peanut oil
50 ml Port wine

500 g butter
Salt and pepper
4 filets mignons
100 ml brown veal stock

Using a small amount of peanut oil in a copper saucepan, heat the filets mignons on both sides. Salt and pepper the filets and cook to taste. Remove the filets and keep them in a warm place. Remove the remaining juices from the pan and heat, without discolouring, the chopped shallots. Add the sliced mushrooms. Mix the mushrooms well with the shallots and then add the Port. Reduce by half and add the veal stock. Cook this mixture for several minutes and salt and pepper to taste. Add the butter in small pieces to bind the sauce, then pour over the warm filets mignons.

This dish can be served with shallot conserves, sautéed spinach or soufflé potatoes. Serves 4.

Mohamed Al Fayed, Harrods, London

NIGEL'S PASTA BAKE

My favourite food is, of course, Cornish Pasty, but I am sending you a pasta recipe – this may be healthier!

1 smoked sausage
1 jar tomato sauce/sieved tin of tomatoes/passata
½ tsp mixed herbs
6 oz pasta shapes
4 oz mushrooms
2 oz grated cheese, plus 2 oz to sprinkle on the top

Cook pasta till ready. Chop up sausage, courgette and mushrooms and add to cooked pasta. Add 2 oz grated cheese, tomato sauce and herbs. Mix well, put into an ovenproof dish and sprinkle rest of cheese on top. Bake in oven Gas Mark4/180°C for about 30 minutes. This is a quick and very tasty meal. Even I can cook it, so it must be easy! Enjoy!

Nigel Martyn, Leeds United FC

CORNED BEEF HASH

It was lovely to hear from someone in Cornwall. In fact my mum came from just up the road from you – Caharrack. Her surname being Tredre and I believe there's a family grave in the churchyard there. So as you might imagine I grew up on some rather special Cornish pasties.

However, for your book I'll give you my recipe for "Corned Beef Hash". I'm a keen offshore sailor so something that's easy to cook in a cramped/moving galley and satisfies a hungry crew is always popular. On a warm day it can be served with a green salad but when it's cold a tin of baked beans will do. For that extra "kick" you can always add some Worcestershire sauce. So you'll need

1 tin corned beef	*1 onion*
4 or 5 cooked potatoes	*Milk*
Salt and pepper	*Dried mixed herbs*

Chop the onion, potatoes and corned beef. Fry the onion in some oil and when it's cooked add the potatoes, corned beef with salt, pepper and mixed herbs to taste. Warm the mixture through by turning then add a little milk to the pan. Leave on a low heat until it browns underneath. Turn out onto plates and add your chosen accompaniment. Bon appétit and best wishes.

Peter Cockroft
BBC Weather Presenter

WELSH POTATO CAKES
WITH LEEKS, CHEESE AND BACON

The leek is the national emblem of Wales – it goes back to early times when Celts in battle used to wear the leek to distinguish themselves from the enemy!

1 kg potatoes (King Edward's or Desirée)
Salt, black pepper
75 g butter, plus a bit extra
1 medium egg
125 g plain flour, extra to dust
3 good sized leeks, cleaned and sliced
150 g Caerphilly cheese, grated
Bacon to serve

Boil, drain and mash the potatoes with 50g of the butter. Season well, then beat in the egg and flour. Melt remaining butter and cook the sliced leeks until tender and just beginning to brown (about 10 minutes). Cool, then season well and stir in the cheese.

Separate the potato mixture into 8 portions. With floured hands form the portions into balls. Make a deep dent in each and add a good spoonful of the leek and cheese mixture, then reform the ball to totally enclose the filling. Flatten each to make a cake about two thirds of a centimetre deep, dust each side with flour.

Heat a griddle or heavy-based frying pan over a medium heat and grease with a little butter. Cook the potato cakes for about 5-8 minutes on each side, until each side is golden brown. Serve with bacon if wished, or else with a salad and some chutney. Delicious!

Keith Atkinson, Director
Camborne School of Mines

SHANGHAI'D CHICKEN

Small chicken breasts, skinless and boned
1½ oz broccoli cut into small pieces
3 oz mushrooms sliced
1 dessertspoon cornflour
1 dessertspoon of soy sauce
1½ tbsp oil
1 small onion chopped
1 clove garlic chopped
1 tsp fresh grated ginger
½ tsp salt
2 tbsp sherry with 1 tbsp water
2 spring onions chopped

Cut the chicken into fine pieces. Put in bowl and sprinkle with cornflour and mix well. Sprinkle with soy sauce. Leave to marinade for 30 minutes. Heat 1 tsp of oil in frying pan or wok. When very hot stir-fry chicken for 2 minutes. Put on plate and keep warm. Add ½ tbsp of oil to pan, add onion, garlic and ginger. Cook for 2 mins, add broccoli, mushrooms and salt and stir fry for 1min. Add chicken, turn heat down to medium, pour in sherry and water and half the spring onions. Put lid on pan, cook for 1 min. Serve with rest of spring onion sprinkled over. Enjoy!

Robbie Dee,   Pirate FM102 Radio, Redruth

PORK FILLET WITH APRICOTS AND BEER

For four people. Preparation time 25 minutes. Cooking time 10 minutes.

1 lb pork tenderloin	2 tsp flour
1 onion	½ pint dry light ale
2 oz butter	4 oz ready to eat apricots
1 tbsp grain mustard	¼ pint whipping cream

Trim the tenderloin of all fat and sinew. Cut the medallions ¼ inch thick. Soak the apricots in the beer. (Even though they are no-soak, they still need to absorb the beer flavour.)

Dice the onion very finely. Melt the butter in a heavy-based saucepan and add the onion. Turn down the heat and cook for 15 minutes until soft with no colouring.

Stir the mustard into the onion mix and cook on medium heat for a couple of minutes. Dust the pork medallions with the flour. Turn up the heat and add the pork. Cook quickly until it is browned. Season with salt and pepper.

Add the apricots and beer, bring to the boil stirring occasionally to stop it sticking. Turn down to simmer. Add the cream, bring to the boil and simmer gently to thicken. Adjust the seasoning with a little lemon juice, salt and pepper. Serve with warm buttered noodles.

Mike Maguire
Trengilly Wartha Inn, Constantine, Cornwall

CHILLI CON CARNE

3 lb lean mince	4 chicken stock cubes
Chilli powder to taste	1 lb onions – chopped
1 lb mushrooms – chopped	4 garlic cloves
1 tin red sweet pimentos	¼ bottle tarragon vinegar
3 tbsp cumin - ground	1 tbsp coriander – ground
1 tbsp oregano	3 tins red kidney beans
3 tins tomatoes	Tomato paste
½ bar Meunier cooking chocolate with the green wrapper	

Fry onions in a little olive oil with crushed garlic. Add meat together with all the seasonings. Add the rest of the vegetables. Make up the chicken stock with water and pour over the ingredients, there should be enough to cover.

Add the chocolate and tomato paste.

Gently simmer for about 3 hours – stirring occasionally. Serve with rice or pasta. Grated cheese is also a good addition if sprinkled over top of each portion.

This dish freezes well, and gains strength in flavour.

Wendy Richards
EastEnders

MSAKHAN – CHICKEN SERVED IN BREAD

This recipe comes from the Middle East and makes a lovely meal in the hand. You could call it a Middle Eastern version of the Cornish Pasty! You can serve it with salad and yoghurt. Pitta bread really is necessary for this recipe.

25-40 g or 1-1½ oz butter
2 onions, peeled and chopped
½ tsp ground cinnamon
1 cardamom pod, crushed
4 chicken portions, preferably breast, skinned and boned
2 pitta breads, cut in half

3 tbsp olive oil
Salt and freshly ground black pepper
Juice of half a lemon

Melt the butter and oil together in a frying pan. Add the onions and fry until soft. Add the chicken pieces, salt, pepper, cinnamon, cardamom pod and the lemon juice. Cook gently, turning over the chicken from time to time, for about 15-20 minutes, until the chicken is cooked through and tender but still juicy. Take out the cardamom pod.

Put a piece of chicken in each half pitta bread, with onions and some of the sauce from the frying pan. Put the stuffed pitta breads on a baking sheet and pop them into a hot oven 180°C/350°F/Gas Mark 4 for about 10 minutes.

Keith and Susie Thompson,
who put this book together.

BEEF IN GUINNESS

1 kg/2 lb beef chuck steak, cut into 4 cm/1½ inch cubes
Plain (all-purpose) flour, for coating
45 ml/3 tbsp oil
1 large onion, sliced
1 carrot, thinly sliced
2 celery sticks, thinly sliced
10 ml/2 tsp sugar
5 ml/1 tsp English mustard powder
15 ml/1 tbsp tomato purée (paste)
Three 2.5x7.5 cm strips of orange rind
Bouquet garni
600 ml/1 pint/2½ cups of Guinness
Salt and pepper

Toss the beef in flour to coat. Heat 30 ml/2 tbsp oil in a large, shallow pan, then cook the beef in batches until lightly browned. Transfer to bowl. Add the remaining oil to the pan, then cook the onions until well browned, adding the carrot and celery towards the end.

Stir in the sugar, mustard, tomato purée (paste), orange rind, Guinness and seasoning. Then add the bouquet garni and bring to the boil. Return the meat and any juices in the bowl to the pan. Add water, if necessary, so the meat is covered. Cover the pan tightly and cook gently for 2-2½ hours, until the meat is very tender.

And there you have it – a very wholesome and satisfying meal!
Serves 6.

Victor Obogu
Bath Rugby Union Football Club

YORKSHIRE OPEN BACON AND EGG PIE

Pastry:
6 oz (175 g) plain flour
Pinch of salt
3 oz (75 g) English butter (or half butter/half lard if preferred)
A little cold water to bind

Filling:
1 medium onion, finely chopped
6 oz (175 g) British streaky bacon, chopped
2 large eggs beaten
5 fl oz fresh single cream
Freshly ground black pepper
4 oz (100 g) Mature English Cheddar cheese, grated
Optional: chives cut into about 1 cm lengths

Sift together the flour and salt into a bowl. Rub in the butter (or butter and lard) until the mixture resembles fine breadcrumbs. Add enough cold water to mix to firm dough. Roll out the pastry on a lightly floured work surface and use to line an 8 inch (20.5 cm) loose bottomed flan tin placed on a baking sheet.

In a frying pan, fry the bacon gently in its own fat for 2 to 3 minutes. In the meantime, finely chop the onion and scatter it over the pastry base. Allow the bacon to cool slightly and then place it over onion in pastry case. Scatter the chives over the top if used.

Beat the eggs, fresh cream and freshly ground black pepper together with half the cheese. Pour the mixture into the pastry case and scatter over remaining cheese. Bake in the oven at 220°C/Gas Mark 7 for 10-15 minutes. Reduce to 190°C/Gas Mark 5 and cook for a further 25 to 30 minutes, until set and golden brown. Serve hot or cold. Serves 4 to 6.

The Rt.Hon.William Hague, M.P.

VEGETARIAN

SAUCY BABY VEG

Serves two – ready in ten to fifteen minutes

2 oz mange tout peas
2 oz baby carrots chopped in 1 inch long pieces
2 oz baby sweetcorn chopped into 1 inch long pieces
One medium courgette, sliced
Olive oil
Two tubs of Dolmio stir-in sauce (roasted vegetables)
8 oz of tagliatelle

Put the tagliatelle in a saucepan of salted boiling water and cook according to packet instructions.

Steam the baby carrots and sweetcorn for ten minutes until beginning to soften through. Put the mange tout and courgettes into the next level of the steamer after the first five minutes and steam until softened. So both sets of veggies are about ready at the same time. Then drain the whole lot.

Heat a smidgen of olive oil in a frying pan or wok. Add the drained vegetables and stir gently.

Now the tricky bit. Open the two tubs of Dolmio stir-in sauce and add to the pan/wok and heat through. Meanwhile drain the pasta – pop onto plates – then dollop loads of the lovely sauce on the top. I like Parmesan cheese with mine.

Alison Johns
Westcountry Television

4.   Hide behind a door.

5.   Wait till a turnip comes in.

6.   Say 'boo'!

Baldrick
(As dictated to Tony Robinson)

A DRAWLING
BY
BLADRICK

TOFU STIR FRY

This recipe for Tofu Stir Fry is a real favourite with my children. It's good for them, but they are not bothered about that because it tastes great. It all sounds delicious and I am sure your book will be a huge success.

2 tbsp olive oil
1 pack fresh tofu
1 courgette sliced
1 small bag of beansprouts
6 baby corn on the cob, each cut into 3 pieces
8 baby asparagus spears, left whole
8 button mushrooms, cut into slices

2 tbsp soy sauce
1 tbsp chopped spring onion
2 tsp minced ginger root
¼ pint vegetable stock
1 tbsp sesame oil

Combine the soy sauce, spring onion, ginger, stock and sesame oil in a bowl.

Cut the tofu into strips 1cm x 1cm x 5cm and drain thoroughly.

Put the olive oil into a wok and heat until smoking. Add the tofu to the olive oil and fry until golden brown. Remove from the wok and drain well. Add all the vegetables (except the beansprouts) to the wok and fry for five minutes. Add the beansprouts, tofu and remaining ingredients, bring to the boil and simmer for two minutes.

Serve immediately with plain boiled rice.

Gary Lineker

EDITH'S VEGETARIAN CASSEROLE SUPREME
AS SERVED AT CAFÉ RENÉ

Ingredients for casserole:
12 oz onions – sliced
12 oz mushrooms – sliced
8 hard boiled eggs, shelled and cut in half
3 oz butter
¼ tsp sage, chopped finely
1 tsp lemon juice
Pinch of salt

For the sauce:
1 oz flour
1 oz butter
3 oz grated cheese
¾ pint milk

In a casserole (with a lid). On top of stove. Fry in butter the onions, mushrooms, sage, salt and lemon juice till cooked.

Make the sauce: Melt butter – add flour, stirring well. Gradually add milk still stirring to avoid lumps. Cook for about a minute – stir in cheese.

Place the halved eggs over the casserole dish and pour over the cheese sauce. Cover with lid and bake in oven at 350°F/Gas Mark 4 for 45 minutes.

Serves 4, or 6 to 8 as a starter or savoury.

Carmen Silvera

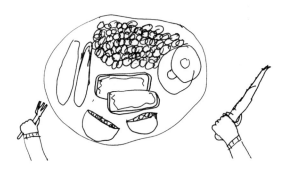

RICE SALAD

Red peppers – chopped
Spring onions – chopped
Cooked rice
Raisins
Cashew Nuts

Dressing
> 3 fl oz olive oil
> 2 tbsp soy sauce
> 1 clove garlic – crushed
> Salt and pepper

Whisk the ingredients for the dressing and then pour over the peppers, spring onions, rice and raisins. Add cashew nuts just before serving.

Dr Mark Porter

CRUNCHY DATE SALAD

2 green skinned apples, quartered and cored
Juice of half a lemon
Half a red pepper, diced
3 sticks of celery, chopped
75 g (3 oz) sun dried stoned dates, chopped
30 ml (2 tbsp) olive oil
5 ml (1 tsp) Dijon mustard
Sea salt and freshly ground black pepper
50 g (2 oz) Cheddar cheese, finely diced

Chop the apples and dip in lemon juice. Drain and mix in with the red pepper, celery and dates.

Whisk together the oil with 10ml (2 tsp) of lemon juice, mustard, salt and pepper. Pour over salad and toss well. Carefully stir in the cheese. Serve on a bed of chicory leaves. Serves 4 to 6.

Darcey Bussell

PAN HAGGERTY

This dish probably has its origins in the North of England and was a popular 'stretching' recipe during the slump. Serves 4. Cooking time 30–40 minutes.

1½ lb cooked potatoes   *3 oz dripping*
1 large onion   *Salt and pepper*
4-6 oz grated cheese

Cut the cooked potatoes into thin slices. Peel and finely chop onion. Heat half the dripping in a large frying pan, add onion and cook until soft, about 3 minutes. Remove and drain onions, add remaining dripping to the pan, and arrange layers of potato, onion and cheese in the pan, seasoning each layer with plenty of salt and pepper. Cover and cook for 15-20 minutes. Remove lid and brown under a hot grill. Pan Haggerty can either be turned out or served straight from the pan.

Variations:
Cook 2 oz finely chopped bacon with the onions.
Add a layer of chopped chicken, ham or meat when cooking the Pan Haggerty.

Robin and Louella Hanbury-Tenison
(Original recipe from a recipe book written by Marika Hanbury-Tenison)

SUNNY WEATHER SPAGHETTI

Spaghetti
Lemon juice - 2 lemons max
Olive oil - a very good glug of oil
Parmesan – grated - a good big chunk
Fresh basil – garnish
Black pepper – to season

In a bowl mix together the oil and lemon juice, then stir in the grated Parmesan so it 'melts'.

Once the spaghetti is cooked, drain it and plonk on the Parmesan mixture. Give it a good mix around so that everything is coated.

Grind on some fresh pepper and sprinkle on some broken basil leaves.

I love this. A good glass of white wine is pretty crucial too!

Isobel Lang
BBC Weather Centre

PASTA WITH TWO CHEESES

Serves two.

1 large tin (15 oz/375 g) plum tomatoes
1 clove garlic, chopped
1 tbsp olive oil (or any oil)
2 tsp dried basil or five fresh basil leaves
2 oz/50 g mature Cheddar cheese, grated
5 oz/125 g Mozzarella cheese chopped into cubes
Any sort of pasta!

Put a large pan of slightly salted water on to boil. In a heavy- based pan, mash the tomatoes with the back of a wooden spoon, add the oil, basil and garlic and simmer gently so that the sauce thickens. When the water boils, add the pasta, following the cooking instructions on the pack. It normally takes ten minutes for pasta to be ready.

Now add the two cheeses to the tomato sauce, turning the heat right down. Stir well once, and then leave while the pasta is finished off. If the sauce starts to stick, turn the heat down and cover with a lid to keep it hot.

Rt. Hon Paddy Ashdown, MP

MIDGELEY'S PERFECT PASTA SAUCE

This is a simple, but completely authentic, Italian tomato sauce. It serves two to three people.

1 tbsp extra virgin olive oil
1 clove garlic - crushed
Handful of chopped fresh rosemary
1 x 400 g tin chopped tomatoes
Handful chopped fresh parsley
Handful chopped fresh basil
Chilli powder to taste
Glass of red wine
Salt and freshly ground black pepper
Penne (pasta quills)
Knob of butter
Parmesan cheese

Heat the oil and gently fry the garlic and rosemary for three to four minutes. Add tomatoes, chilli, wine, salt and pepper and simmer until well reduced – about half an hour. Five minutes before the end of cooking time add parsley and basil, saving a little for serving. Cook the pasta al dente, 12 – 15 minutes, drain and add knob of butter and pepper. Mix in the tomato sauce and serve with the Parmesan cheese and herbs.

Louise Midgley
Westcountry Television

SELSEY RAREBIT

Take a slice of bread. Toast on one side.

Chop some cheese. Butter the untoasted side of the bread, and put on the cheese, adding tomato, salt and pepper if required.

Grill till it is brown and bubbling.

Eat.

Two Selsey Rarebits, clapped together on the cheesy side make
ONE MARTIAN PANCAKE.   Enjoy it – and best wishes!

Patrick Moore, CBE, FRAS

"PUKE ON A PLATE"

Knob of butter
Four slices of toast
½ lb grated cheese
8 sliced ripe tomatoes

Melt knob of butter in frying pan. Add sliced tomatoes and stir for a few minutes to soften tomatoes. Add grated cheese and allow to melt. Pour over toast.

Ross Kemp
EastEnders

THE CHIP BUTTIE

This has to be one of my favourite recipes, it's also very easy to make ...

Take two thick slices of crusty white bread. Spread both slices generously with plenty of butter.

Now fill with sizzling hot, fresh fried chips. Season to taste.

EAT IMMEDIATELY !!

Terry Wogan OBE

FROM MY GARDEN

I am no cook, but enjoy my vegetables. I like to go out and gather two or three vegetables – peas, cabbage, leeks. Then I prepare and cook the peas. While I'm eating these, the cabbage and leeks are cooked together, and eaten as a second course (on the same plate). Finish with fresh strawberries or raspberries.

Rosemary Verey
Gardening Writer

BOND STREET VEGETABLE "THING"

This recipe came about when health problems required a low fat/healthy eating diet. It is one of our answers to the cry that "low fat equals no taste", and has become a favourite with many of our visitors, vegetarian and meat eaters alike. There are many variations to this recipe but this is our favourite "thing".

1 lb potatoes cut into 1 inch cubes
½ lb carrots, cubed
½ lb swede, cubed
2 medium parsnips, cubed
1 large onion, roughly chopped
2 garlic cloves (or more if taste and friends permit)
1 large tin tomatoes mashed
1 tin mixed bean salad
Olive oil

Steam the first four ingredients until slightly undercooked. Meanwhile, gently soften the onion and garlic with a little oil in a pan, then add the tin of tomatoes and bring to the boil. (This makes a very tasty sauce – but if health is not an issue you could use a pasta sauce in place of the tomatoes.)

Lightly grease a large ovenproof dish with olive oil and add the steamed vegetables. Then mix in the beans. Finally, pour the tomato mixture over the top, cover with foil and bake in a moderate oven until all the vegetables are cooked.

This gives two large servings or will serve four as a dish which goes very well with gammon steaks! For a more "Mediterranean" dish we use about one and a half pounds in total of peppers, courgettes and aubergines with the potatoes, and more garlic!

Peter Bishop,
The Bond Street Optician

QUICK PASTA

Serves 4.

1 onion
1 tin of sweetcorn drained, large or small according to taste
500 g dried pasta shapes – shells, bows or twists
125 g grated Cheddar cheese
A drizzle of corn oil
A pinch of salt

Pour two litres of water into a large saucepan and add a little oil and a pinch of salt. Bring to the boil. When boiling add the dried pasta, stir and return to the boil. Cook for 10 minutes.

Whilst the pasta is cooking, chop the onion into small pieces. In another saucepan put a little oil and add the onion. When the onion is nearly cooked add the sweetcorn. Cook gently on a low heat.

When the pasta is cooked, drain and place in a large bowl. Add the cooked onion and sweetcorn and the grated cheese. Mix together well and serve immediately.

Sandra Togneri
School Support Staff

NACHOS

Hungry and looking for a fast snack? Make these nibbles instead of opening a packet of crisps. For 6 to 8.

5 oz (150 g) tortilla chips
8 oz (250 g) mild Cheddar cheese, grated
6 tbsp bottled hot taco sauce (optional)

Spread the tortilla chips one layer deep in shallow baking dishes. Sprinkle with the cheese and dot the optional sauce on top. Bake at 200°C/400°F/Gas Mark 6 for 5 minutes. Cool until approachable, serve immediately and eat at once!

Trudi Temple
School Support Staff

BACHELOR SCRAMBLED EGGS AND TOMATOES

You need:
Two eggs and one tomato per person (maybe a spring onion if you like them). Bits of milk, butter, salt and pepper.

First melt a small splodge of butter (or margarine) in frypan and drop in finely cut up spring onion … cook over slow heat for a short while – then add a slosh of milk – too much and eggs are watery later. Take pan off the heat while you break eggs into pan. Add a dusting of salt to each egg and as much pepper as you enjoy.

Then, back on to low heat while you graunch up the eggs with a wooden spoon and generally scramble them around. Must be low heat – nothing is worse than little black horribly tasting burnt bits in scrambled egg.

Meanwhile – your tomato should be cut in half and placed under overhead grill. Put flat side down first and grill until skin shrivels and starts to go black. Then turn over, add dusting of salt and grill the flat side.

Your scrambled egg should be just starting to solidify, so take it off the heat for a tick while you pop in your two beautifully grilled tomatoes. The skin on the smooth side just comes away but you will need to cut out the core on the other half of the tomato.

Back on the heat while you squelch up the tomato with the wooden spoon. Don't dry it up too much – delicious. (Mix egg and tomato thoroughly.)

Rolf Harris

YORKSHIRE PUDDING

Pre-heat oven to Gas Mark 7/425°F/220°C.

250 g or 8 oz plain flour
Pinch of salt
3 eggs
Up to 600 ml or 1 pint milk, or half milk/half water
Fat or oil

Sift the flour and the salt into a largish bowl. Make a well in the middle and break the eggs into it. Add a little milk. Beginning at the centre, stir these ingredients into a batter, gradually pouring in the remainder of the milk, or milk and water. An electric whisk will do this very quickly. The amount of milk, or milk and water, will depend on the size of the eggs. The batter should be of a creamy but pouring consistency.

Put the fat or oil into an ovenproof tin, and put it in the oven to pre-heat. Take the tin from the oven and pour the batter into it. It helps if you put the hot tin onto a heated ring or burner on the top of the stove to keep it really hot, so that the batter sizzles as it drops into the hot fat. Put the tin back in the oven, on a shelf towards the top. Bake for 25-30 minutes, when it should be risen, crisp and golden.

Jeremy Guscott
Bath Rugby Union Football Club

PASS DA TOMATO!

As a newspaper editor I am asked to do many things, but your request for a recipe is a first! I hope the following will be of some use. As a mere male, I find that cooking is a daunting task; a bit like editing a newspaper – there seem to be so many things that can go wrong! However, there is one simple dish which I have mastered and now enjoy (as do our two Jack Russell terriers when I make too much).

This recipe was shown to me by my 14 year old daughter, Hannah, with these words: "Dad, this one is so simple even you can't mess it up!" We call it Pass Da Tomato:

The main ingredients are pasta and tomato (clever, eh) and a large onion. Here's what you do: peel the onion and slice it into whatever size pieces you prefer. Heat a tablespoonful of oil in a pan, add the pieces of onion and fry for about five minutes, or until they are soft and brown. Add a medium size tin of tomatoes to the oil and onions and heat gently for about ten minutes.

Cook enough pasta for two people (in our house that's usually a whole packet!), serve on a warm plate and add the tomato and onion mix. This provides a basic pasta meal to which you can add virtually anything, from chicken to prawns. Even on its own it's a tasty snack or starter.

John Pearn
Editor of The West Briton

LEEK, EGG AND CHEESE PUFFS

8 oz leeks, washed and sliced
Salt
1 tsp vegetable oil
1 small onion, peeled and sliced
Freshly ground black pepper
½ tsp coriander seeds, crushed
3 oz Wensleydale cheese cut into small cubes
2 hard boiled eggs, shelled and halved lengthways
I egg, beaten
Frozen puff pastry, defrosted and cut into 4 pieces, each 4 inch square

Cook the leeks in boiling salted water for 3 minutes or until just tender. Drain and allow to cool. Heat oil in a small pan and fry the onion until lightly browned. Add salt, pepper, coriander seeds and leeks. Cook for a further minute. Allow to cool for 10 minutes, then stir in the cheese.

Brush the edges of the pastry squares with beaten egg. Divide the filling evenly between the squares, placing it just off-centre, and top with half a boiled egg. Fold over the pastry to make a triangle. Seal the edges firmly and brush the tops with beaten egg.

Bake for 15-20 minutes at 220°C/425°F/Gas Mark 7, until puffed up and golden brown. Serve hot with a crisp green salad, or leave to cool to make a good picnic or packed lunch dish. Serves 4.

Wallace and Gromit
With a little help from Nick Park!

PUDDINGS

CANDY'S CHOCOLATE MOUSSE

2 oz plain chocolate
1 egg, separated
1 dessertspoon of rum or your favourite liqueur

To serve:
1 fl oz (25 ml) pouring cream
Grated chocolate (good quality)

Start off by setting a small basin over a pan of barely simmering water. Break up the chocolate into small pieces (no nibbles!), add these to the basin and stir till the chocolate has melted.

Next separate the egg, the white into a medium-sized bowl and the yolk into a smaller one. Beat up the yolk then stir it well into the chocolate mixture, off the heat. Now stir your liqueur into it, and leave to cool for about 10 minutes.

Meanwhile whisk up the egg white and then using a metal spoon fold the egg white into the chocolate mixture. Spoon the whole lot into a stemmed wineglass, cover with clingfilm and chill for a couple of hours. To serve: Pour the cream over the top of the mousse and sprinkle with a little grated chocolate.

EAT! ENJOY!

Candy Atherton, our local MP

DAWN'S CHOCOLATE FRUIT FONDUE

Melt three Mars Bars, or a Terry's Chocolate Orange, in a glass heatproof dish over a pan of hot water. Add a tiny bit of milk.

Chop up fruit - apples, pears, oranges, bananas, tangerines, etc.

Dip the pieces of fruit in the hot melted chocolate.

Enjoy!

Dawn French

TWICE BAKED CHOCOLATE SOUFFLÉS

100 g/4 oz plain chocolate (70% cocoa solids)
225 ml/8 fl oz milk
50 g/2 oz unsalted butter, plus extra for greasing
4 tbsp plain flour
4 large eggs, separated
6 tbsp caster sugar, plus extra for dusting
2 tbsp sifted cocoa powder
300 ml/½ pint double cream
Icing sugar, to dust
Crème fraîche to serve

Preheat the oven to 375°F/190°C/Gas Mark 5. Melt the chocolate in a heatproof bowl set over a pan of simmering water. Heat the milk in a pan until just at boiling point. Remove from the heat and stir in half the melted chocolate.

Melt the butter in a small pan and stir in the flour and cook over a low heat for 1 minute. Remove from the heat and gradually add the milk and chocolate mixture, stirring until smooth after each addition. Return to the heat and cook for a few minutes, stirring until smooth and shiny. Transfer to a large bowl with a spatula; leave to cool a little.

Add the egg yolks one at a time to the chocolate sauce and mix. Whisk the egg whites until soft peaks form. Add four tablespoons of the sugar and whisk again for 30 seconds, then fold in half the cocoa powder. Lightly beat a third of the egg whites into the chocolate mixture until blended. Add the rest of the egg whites and gently fold in. Divide between 4 x 225ml or 8 fl oz buttered and sugared ramekins. Place on a baking sheet and bake for 15-20 minutes until well risen and a light crust has formed.

Place the cream in a small pan with the remaining sugar and melted chocolate, and whisk in. Mix the remaining cocoa powder with a little water to make a paste and stir into the pan. Simmer for a few minutes.

Remove the soufflés from the oven and quickly tip then out of the ramekins into an ovenproof dish, right side up. Pour over the chocolate sauce and bake for 10-15 minutes until well risen and the sauce is bubbling. Transfer the soufflés to serving plates, stir the sauce and spoon around the soufflés. Dust with icing sugar and add a quenelle of crème fraîche. Serves 4.

Antony Worrall Thompson
Celebrity Chef

JURASSIC JELLY - INSECTS IN AMBER TRIFLE!

About thirty million years ago, many insects got stuck in a sticky patch! They were trapped by the treacly resin of coniferous trees, while crawling about on them. More and more resin oozed out over them until they had no way of escaping. Sometimes this resin became fossilised as beautiful, yellowy-orange material, amber, with the insect still inside. Not all amber contains an insect, but it can contain insects that are now extinct. Amber is one of the only ways that insects can be preserved over many years; they usually decay before they can be preserved in rocks, so amber is a very precious timepiece, for nature lovers and jewellery lovers!

½ cup orange juice
1 small pack liquorice allsorts
1 liquorice bootlace
1 pint milk
Sugar to sprinkle

1 pack trifle sponges
1 packet chocolate blancmange
1 pack orange jelly
25 g marzipan

Your jelly needs to be set before you start your trifle so do this the day before, following the instructions on the packet.

Find a container for your trifle (a see-through one is best). Break up the trifle sponge so that it covers the base of the container. Pour the orange juice over the sponge evenly to keep it moist. Allow the blancmange to set slightly and then pour over the sponges. Sprinkle some sugar over it to prevent a skin forming. Now spoon on the jelly so that it covers the surface. Use little spoonfuls to make it easier.

Lastly make the insects. Use the marzipan to make the bodies. 25g will be enough for about 3 insects. You can mould the body into shape. By cutting and slicing the liquorice allsorts you can make wings, compound eyes, antennae and even stripy bees' bodies! Make your insect by pushing the body parts into the marzipan. Then give your insect 6 legs using the liquorice bootlaces. 1cm is enough for each leg, push these into the marzipan body. Now "trap" your insects in resin by placing them into your jelly. If you want to entomb your insects, and you like jelly, you might want to cover them with more jelly!

Cornwall Wildlife Trust

58

PEACH BRULÉE

6 fresh peaches, peeled halved and stoned
½ tsp (1 x 2.5 ml) ground cinnamon
½ pint (300 ml) double or whipping cream, chilled
1 oz (25 g) icing sugar, sifted
6 oz (175 g) demerara sugar

Put the peach halves, cut side down, in a single layer in a shallow, heatproof dish. Sprinkle with the cinnamon. Whip the cream and icing sugar together until thick, then spread over the peaches. Sprinkle the demerara sugar over the cream to cover it completely, then put under a preheated, moderate grill for a few minutes, until the topping is dark and bubbling.

Remove from the heat, leave until cold, then chill in the refrigerator for at least two hours before serving. Serve chilled. Serves 4-6.

Jimmy Young

SUMMER PUDDING

750 g soft fresh fruit
100-175 g granulated sugar, or to taste
About 9 thick slices white bread from a small tin loaf, crusts removed

Put the fruit in a heavy pan with sugar to taste and heat gently for 2 to 3 minutes until the sugar is dissolved, shaking the pan constantly. (Do not stir or overcook or the fruit will lose its shape.) Remove from heat and leave to cool.

Meanwhile line the base and sides of a 1½ pint pudding basin with bread, making sure there are no gaps between the slices. Pour in the fruit, and then cover the top completely with bread and press down firmly.

Place a saucer on top to just fit inside the basin tightly, then place heavy weights on top. Chill in fridge overnight, then turn out onto a serving plate. Serve chilled with cream.

Any combination of fruits will do – raspberries, redcurrants, blackcurrants or blackberries or one fruit according to which is most plentiful.

Karen Brokenshire
Headteacher

BANANA SPLITS WITH HOT CHOCOLATE SAUCE

For each person you will need
One large banana
2-3 spoonfuls ice cream
1 tbsp hot chocolate sauce (see recipe below)
1 tbsp thick cream
Grated chocolate and/or nuts for decorating

Peel and cut the banana in half lengthways, then put it in a bowl or on a plate. Put the ice cream between the two pieces of banana. Pour the hot chocolate sauce over the top. Top with the cream and decorate with nuts or chocolate on the top.

HOT CHOCOLATE SAUCE

50 g (2 oz) chocolate bar *1 tbsp brown sugar*
1 tbsp cold water *25 g (1 oz) butter*

Put the chocolate, sugar and water into a small saucepan over a low heat. Stir until the chocolate melts and the mixture is smooth and creamy. Remove from the heat. Add the butter in small lumps and beat well. Pour over the banana splits as in the recipe above. It's also very good poured over plain vanilla ice-cream.

Antoine Sampson
Teacher Class 6

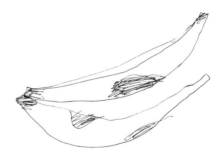

LEMON DELIGHT

2 tbsp butter *2 eggs*
¾ cup sugar (breakfast cup) *1 lemon*
1 cup milk (breakfast cup) *2 tbsp flour*

Cream butter and sugar, add well-beaten yolks, flour and lemon juice. Add milk and stiffly beaten whites of eggs. Put into greased dish and stand in pan of boiling water for 65 minutes in moderate oven.

My family all love this pudding.

Lady Mary Holborow JP
Lord Lieutenant of Cornwall

BREAD AND BUTTER PUDDING

½ pint (275 ml) milk
⅛ pint (70 ml) double cream
Grated rind of half a small lemon
2 oz (50 g) castor sugar
3 eggs
Pannetone cake, brioche or white bread
½ oz (10 g) candied lemon or orange peel, finely chopped
2 oz (50 g) currants
Freshly grated nutmeg

Heat oven to Gas Mark 4/350°F/180°C.

Butter a 2 pint (1 litre) oblong enamel baking dish. Slice the Pannetone, brioche or bread and butter it. Put one layer on the base of the dish, sprinkle with the candied peel and half the currants. Put another layer of Pannetone, brioche or bread in the dish and sprinkle with the rest of the currants.

Put the milk and cream together in a measuring jug, stir in the lemon peel and sugar. Whisk the eggs in a small basin and add to the milk mixture. Pour the whole lot over the contents of the baking dish and sprinkle with freshly grated nutmeg. Bake in the oven for 30-40 minutes. Serve warm.

This is delicious and provides the perfect solution for what to do with those dry Italian cakes you get given at Christmas!

Dame Judi Dench

FRESH FRUIT ICE CREAM

½ lb raspberries, strawberries, peaches or nectarines
4 oz (110 g) castor sugar
2 egg yolks
2 egg whites
¼ pint (150 ml) double cream

Stew fruit for 2-3 minutes with sprinkling of sugar. Push raspberries through sieve. The other fruits can be puréed in a blender. Cool.

Beat egg whites until stiff with half the sugar. Beat yolks with 1oz (25g) sugar until creamy and fold into the beaten whites. Beat the cream with remaining sugar until slightly thickened. Fold into the egg mixture. Add puréed fruit and fold thoroughly, lifting from the bottom to prevent the fruit from sinking. Freeze. Remove to refrigerator one hour before serving.

**Susan, Lady St Levan
St Michael's Mount, Cornwall**

FRUIT SALAD

2 apples	2 pears
2 peaches/mangoes	Half a melon
2 kiwi fruit	2 bananas

Handful of grapes, cherries, strawberries
Half a lemon
Half an orange
Sherry and sugar to taste

Peel, chop and remove the cores or pips/seeds from the above fruit. Put into a big salad bowl.

Squeeze in lemon juice and orange juice and add some sugar or alcohol (e.g. sherry) to taste. Leave to settle. Refrigerate. Serve with cream or ice cream. Serves 4-6.

ENJOY!!!

**Michael Buerk
BBC TV News Presenter**

63

APPLE AND RHUBARB ALMOND SPONGE

1 lb cooking apples
Grated rind and juice of 1 orange
3 oz Demerara sugar

1 lb rhubarb
2 oz sultanas

Sponge

3 oz butter
2 eggs
3 oz self-raising flour
Pinch salt
Flaked almonds

3 oz sugar
A few drops almond essence
1 oz ground almonds
A little milk

Peel and slice the apples. Wash and cut rhubarb into 1-inch pieces. Put in a saucepan with orange juice and rind, sugar and sultanas. Simmer for about 15 minutes. Pour into greased ovenproof dish.

For the sponge topping. Cream the butter and sugar. Add the eggs and almond essence. Mix in flour, ground almonds and salt. Add a little milk to make a dropping consistency. Then spoon over the fruit and sprinkle the top with flaked almonds. Cook at 180^{0}C/Gas Mark 4 for 35-40 minutes.

Serve hot with custard or cream.

Richard Branson
Virgin Management Ltd

PASSION FRUIT WATER ICE

1 pint water
8 oz caster sugar
1 egg white
8 passion fruit

Dissolve the sugar in the water over a low heat. Boil gently for 10 minutes. Leave to cool.

Cut passion fruits in half and scoop out the flesh, put in a fine sieve and pass through leaving all the black pips behind. Add juice to cooled sugar syrup and pour into container. Place in freezer and leave until just beginning to freeze around the edges. Add whisked egg white and return to freezer.

I serve this delicious water ice in pretty wineglasses with a wafer biscuit on the top.

Sally Gunnell

FAVOURITES PUDDING

Slice your favourite sponge cake and arrange in your favourite dish.

Smear with your favourite jam and optional berries in season.

Pour over your favourite melted ice cream to moisten the pudding.

Keep for a couple of hours in the fridge and serve to your favourite guests.

Sir Ian McKellen

CHOCOLATE POTS

I'm quite certain that if you eat it quickly, the calories really don't have a chance to take hold. It's quick, simple and wickedly delicious.

½ pint single cream
7 oz dark chocolate
1 tbsp brandy or rum
1 egg
1 tsp sugar

Break chocolate into small pieces. Put in food processor. Add egg and sugar. Process. Heat cream to scalding point. Pour on chocolate mixture while the machine is still running. Add rum or brandy. Spoon into little ramekins or dishes. Refrigerate to eat.

Vanessa Feltz

MINCEMEAT SANDWICHES
FRIED IN BATTER

4 slices of white bread
Mincemeat
Vegetable oil
Batter mix

Spread bread with mincemeat thickly and sandwich together.
Cover with batter.
Plunge into a pan full of hot vegetable oil for a few minutes until golden brown.
Serve hot with cream or ice cream.

Emily Haines
Teacher, Class 3

TABB'S SPICED TOOTI-FRUITI
ICE-CREAM PUDDING

4 egg yolks	*2 oz black treacle*
1 oz golden syrup	*1 oz dark brown sugar*
4 fl oz milk	*6 fl oz double cream*
1 oz raisins	*1 oz currants*
1 oz sultanas	*2 oz chopped glacé cherries*
1 oz mixed peel	*Juice and zest of 2 limes*
3 tbsp sweet vermouth	*½ nutmeg, grated*
½ tsp mixed spice	

Combine raisins, currants, sultanas, cherries, lime juice and zest, vermouth and spices in a glass bowl. Cover and leave in a fridge for 24 hours.

Mix together egg yolks, sugar, syrup and treacle with the milk and place in a saucepan over a low heat, stirring constantly until the mixture becomes a fairly thick custard. DO NOT BOIL. Remove from heat, place in a bowl and whisk vigorously until completely cold – a machine is best for this.

Whisk double cream until it forms stiff peaks and then add fruit mixture, lightly folding it in with a large spoon. Combine cream mixture with beaten custard again, lightly folding it in with a large spoon.

Place mixture in either 6 individual size bowls (¼ pint) or one large container and freeze for 24 hours. Individual bowls can be turned out to serve or use a scoop from the larger container. This goes well with chocolate sauce or cream, and should serve 6 people.

For the chocolate sauce:
2 oz dark chocolate   *Teaspoon sugar*
2 fl oz milk   *Brandy to taste (optional)*

Melt chocolate in a pan over hot water, then add boiled milk and sugar. Allow to cool, then add as much brandy as you like!

Nigel and Melanie Tabb
Tabbs's Restaurant, Portreath, Cornwall

SUMMERTIME STRAWBERRY BLISS

2 lb ripe strawberries
About 8 tbsp icing sugar, or to taste
½ pint chilled double cream
¼ pint chilled single cream
6 meringues, either bought or home made
Brandy or one of the fruit liqueurs – Grand Marnier, Kirsch, etc (optional)

Clean and hull the strawberries. Choose about a dozen of the best looking ones for decoration. Chop the remaining strawberries very roughly and put them in a bowl and sprinkle the icing sugar over the top. Sprinkle with the brandy if you are using it. Mix very gently, cover and put in the fridge for an hour.

The next stage you need to do immediately before serving - this means you have to retire to the kitchen for a few minutes after the main course, leaving your guests wondering! In a large bowl combine the two chilled creams, and beat gently until they hold their shape in soft peaks. Very gently but thoroughly fold the strawberries and all their juices into the cream. Crush the meringues in the palm of your hand and drop them into the strawberry cream. Again, fold into the mixture very lightly. Taste and add more sugar if necessary.

Pile the cream into a large glass serving bowl. Decorate the top with the whole strawberries you put aside earlier, and serve. Serves 6-8. Bliss!!

Catherine Sullivan
Teacher, Class 4

YE OLDE BREDDE PUDDINGE

1 large sliced loaf of bread
1 lb mixed dried fruit
4 tbsp mixed spice
4 oz brown sugar
1 tbsp black treacle (optional)

Break bread down into small pieces. Soak it slightly in warm water until it will bind together. Make sure that the bread doesn't become too moist.
Add the sugar, mixed spice and black treacle to the bread in a bowl and mix well.

Bake in shallow, greased tins in the coolest part of the oven, set at 180°C, for one to one and a half hours. When it is cool, turn it out of the tins. You can serve it on its own, or with custard.

Dean Shipton
Captain of Cornwall RFU team
County Championship winners 1999

LEMON PUDDING

3 fresh eggs
3 lemons
400 g tin condensed milk
1 packet trifle sponges
1 large carton double cream, whipped

Whip eggs until thick and frothy. Add the condensed milk. Cut the lemon in half and take one slice from it. Add the juice of three lemons to the mixture, saving the extra slice. Finely grate a little of the lemon peel and add to the mixture. Mix well.

Take one packet of trifle sponges and break into cubes. Place in the bottom of a glass bowl. Pour the mixture over the sponge. Refrigerate for 20 minutes. Take the bowl from the fridge and pour the whipped cream over the sponge, add a slice of lemon to the top and refrigerate again. Refrigerate for at least two hours. Consume within 24 hours.

Myra Whitney
School Support Staff

TEA-TIME TREATS

COLORADO GIANT COOKIES

75 g butter
50 g white granulated sugar
100 g soft brown sugar
2 eggs
1 tsp vanilla essence
250 g plain flour
½ tsp salt
1 tsp bicarbonate of soda
150 g chocolate chips

Cream together butter, sugar and vanilla essence until smooth then add the eggs and mix well. Sift the flour with bicarbonate of soda and salt and add gradually to the mixture.

Put the mixture in the refrigerator for 20 minutes while you clean up! Pre-heat your oven to 375°F/190°C/Gas Mark 5. Prepare a baking tray either by greasing well or using a sheet of greaseproof paper.

Shape the mixture into small balls using a tablespoon or ice cream scoop and arrange on your baking tray, you should get about 16. Lightly press down on each one with the ball of your hand - don't flatten them completely.

Put in the oven for 7-8 minutes and then let them cool for at least 5 minutes before you eat them.

The Presenters of Blue Peter

NO 10'S ALL IN ONE CHOCOLATE SPONGE

110 g self-raising flour (sifted)
1 tsp baking powder
110 g soft margarine, at room temperature
110 g caster sugar
2 large eggs
1 tbsp cocoa powder

To finish: Icing sugar, jam and/or fresh cream

Pre-heat the oven to Gas Mark 3/325°F/170°C.

You will need two 18cm sponge tins, no less than 4cm deep, lightly greased and lined with greaseproof paper (also greased) or silicone paper.

Take a large roomy mixing bowl and sift flour and baking powder into it, holding the sieve high to give the flour a good airing. Then simply add all the other ingredients to the bowl, and whisk them – preferably with an electric hand whisk – till thoroughly combined. If the mixture doesn't drop off a wooden spoon easily when tapped on the side of the bowl, then add 1 or 2 teaspoons of tap-warm water, and whisk again.

Now divide the mixture between the two prepared tins, level off and bake on the centre shelf of the oven for about 30 minutes. When cooked leave them in the tins for only about 30 seconds, then loosen the edges by sliding a palette knife all round and turn them out onto a wire cooling rack. Peel off the base papers carefully and, when cool, sandwich them together with jam or lemon curd (or jam and fresh cream), and dust with icing sugar.

Cherie Blair

ANZAC BISCUITS and HOKEY POKEY BISCUITS

The following two biscuit recipes are ever popular amongst New Zealand school children. They are perfect for packed lunches. Anzac itself stands for "Australian, New Zealand Army Corp", the combined forces which fought together with the Allies during the First and Second World Wars.

ANZAC BISCUITS

125 g (4 oz) flour	*100 g (3½ oz) butter or margarine*
150 g (6 oz) sugar	*1 tbsp golden syrup*
1 cup coconut	*½ tsp baking soda*
1 cup rolled oats	*2 tbsp boiling water*
½ cup sultanas or raisins	

Preheat the oven to 180°C/350°F/Gas Mark 4.

In a saucepan melt butter and golden syrup. Dissolve baking soda in boiling water and add to saucepan mixture. Add this to the previously mixed flour, sugar, coconut, rolled oats and sultanas. Stir well. Place in spoonfuls on a greased tray. Bake 15-20 minutes. (They will harden more on cooling.)

HOKEY POKEY BISCUITS

125g (4oz) butter or margarine
½ cup (4 oz) sugar
1 tbsp golden syrup

1 tbsp milk
1½ cups flour
1 tsp baking soda

Preheat oven to 180°C/350°F/Gas Mark 4.

In a saucepan melt butter, sugar, golden syrup and milk together.
Cool to lukewarm and sift in flour and baking soda. Place in balls on lightly
greased tray (or tray lined with baking paper). Flatten with a fork. Bake for 15-20
minutes. (They will harden on cooling.)

Diane Leigh from New Zealand
Cook for Lord and Lady St Levan,
St Michael's Mount, Cornwall

APPLE SHORTCAKE

This recipe is certainly one of our family favourites, and also very popular in this
part of South Yorkshire. It can be eaten hot as a dessert with custard or it can be
eaten cold.

4 oz margarine
3 oz sugar
6 oz SR flour

1 egg
1 lb cooked apples

Cream margarine with sugar. Add beaten egg. Gradually mix in flour, adding no
liquid. Put half mixture into a greased tin and level. Spread on the well-drained
apples, and cover with remaining shortcake. Bake in a moderate oven for about 1
hour. If eating cold, cut into squares and dredge with icing sugar.

Dickie Bird,
Yorkshire County Cricket Club

CHOCOLATEY BISCUITY CAKEY THINGS ...

You will need

1 packet chocolate digestive biscuits
100 g (4 oz) butter or margarine
2 tsp sugar
2 tsp cocoa or 4 tsp drinking chocolate
1 tbsp honey or golden syrup
100 g (4 oz) chocolate bar

Grease a square or round sandwich baking tin. Crush the biscuits with a rolling pin, but not too finely. Put the butter, sugar, cocoa and syrup into a medium sized saucepan and melt slowly over a low heat. Mix in the crushed biscuits, then press this gooey mess into the prepared tin, spread flat and leave to cool for 10 minutes. Melt the chocolate in a Pyrex bowl, stood in some water in a saucepan over a low heat. Pour the chocolate over the biscuit cake, spreading evenly, and leave this to set in the fridge for 30 minutes. Cut into squares.

Mmmmmmmmmmmm … they're yummy !!!

Zoe Ball

OATMEAL COOKIES

8 oz butter/margarine
4 oz plain flour
4 oz castor sugar
8 oz oatmeal
2 oz coconut

Mix ingredients together in a bowl. When it forms a ball remove, and with a rolling pin or your hand roll the mixture out until it is about ¼ inch thick. With a pastry cutter about 2½ inches in diameter cut out your biscuits and place on a baking tray.

Bake in a hot oven approx 180°C for about 20 mins or until golden brown. Decorate with a spot of chocolate and ½ walnut if you wish.

John Hurt

ELIZABETH'S HAZELNUT CHEESECAKE

A quick cheesecake, if Hyacinth threatens to come round!

8 oz digestive biscuits
2 oz butter
2 level tablespoons golden syrup
One 5 oz carton hazelnut yoghurt
½ lb curd cheese
One small carton double cream (whipped)
2 oz caster sugar
A sprinkling of hazel nuts

Mix digestive biscuits and butter together and line a pie dish. Mash the cheese. Mix all the ingredients for the filling. Put in biscuit lining. Sprinkle with hazelnuts.

With any luck the nuts will get under Hyacinth's plate.

Josephine Tewson
Elizabeth in "Keeping Up Appearances"

ZELMA'S STUFFED MONKEYS

I can strongly recommend my mother's recipe for a good, fruity, chewy biscuit.

PASTRY

2 heaped cups of flour   *2 eggs*
2 tsp of baking powder   *1 tsp vanilla essence*
2 tbsp sugar   *1 large tbsp cream*
¼ lb butter

FILLING

½ lb dates   *1 tsp vanilla essence*
¼ lb sultanas   *¼ lb chopped nuts*
¼ lb currants   *1 tbsp butter*
2 tbsp sugar mixed with cinnamon to taste

Place flour, baking powder, sugar and vanilla in basin and rub in butter to fine "breadcrumb" texture. Add eggs and mix into a soft dough for rolling out.
Chop all filling ingredients and mix together. Roll out dough into 4 inch strips.

73

Place filling in one half, wet edge and fold other half over. Brush with milk, and sugar and cinnamon mixture and bake in moderate oven. When cooled cut into squares.

Maureen Lipman

REHEARSAL BISCUITS

My grandmother used to make oatmeal biscuits that were just scrummy. When I was a boy, whenever I stayed with her she would bring a cup of tea and two oatmeal biscuits up to me in bed in the mornings – unbelievable pampering as far as I was concerned. I can still taste those biscuits. Unfortunately I never got the recipe from her before she died, but this recipe is the nearest I've come to it. They're also very good during a break in practising!

3 oz butter	*3 oz raisins*
6 oz soft brown sugar	*½ tsp bicarbonate of soda*
7 oz medium porridge oats	*½ tsp salt*
4 oz wholemeal flour	*1 egg, size 2, beaten*

Gently heat the butter in a saucepan. When it has melted remove it from the heat and let it cool slightly. Measure all the ingredients (apart from the egg) and mix in a bowl. When the butter has cooled slightly stir the beaten egg into the butter. Pour the butter and egg mixture into the bowl with the dry ingredients and stir to a stiff paste.

To make the biscuits, flour your hands and take a small amount of the mixture and roll into a walnut-sized ball in the palm of the hand. Flatten slightly and place on a greased baking tray. Leave a little room between the biscuits so that they don't meld into each other when baking. Bake at 180°C for 10-12 minutes. Place on a wire rack to cool, then place in an airtight tin.

Peter Skellern

HYPATIA'S HEAVENLY CHOCOLATE CAKE

1 cup = 8 ounces

Beat together

> *2 cups sugar*
> *⅔ cup margarine*
> *2 whole eggs*

Add   *1 cup sour milk (1 tsp lemon juice or vinegar in any milk)*

Beat in

> *⅔ cup cocoa*
> *2½ cups white flour*
> *2 tsp bicarbonate of soda*
> *⅓ tsp salt*

Add into whole mix

> *1 cup hot black coffee (can be instant)*
> *1 tsp vanilla essence*

Bake in a greased tin at 350°F/180°C until the cake springs when touched.

Frost with dark chocolate butter frosting – it is devilishly good!

Melissa Hardie
The Hypatia Trust

75

WELSH CAKES

I've chosen this recipe because it reminds me of childhood holidays staying with relatives in South Wales. These are cooked on a griddle, but if this is not available then a heavy-based frying pan will do.

450 g/1 lb self raising flour
A pinch of salt
125 g/4 oz lard
125 g/4 oz margarine
175 g/6 oz granulated sugar
50 g/2 oz currants
1 beaten egg
About 3 tbsp milk
A little extra lard to grease the pan

Sift the flour and salt into a basin. Rub in lard and margarine. Add the sugar and currants. Mix to the consistency of pastry dough with beaten egg and milk. Roll out on a floured board to approximately 7mm or ¼ inch thick. Cut with a 6.5cm or 2½ inch plain scone cutter.

Heat griddle or heavy frying pan and grease it lightly with lard. It is wise to test heat by cooking just one cake on its own. If it is too hot, cakes burn before inside is cooked. Cook cakes on both sides until just golden. Grease pan very lightly between batches. Put on wire rack to cool. Store in an airtight container.

This recipe makes 40 to 50 Welsh Cakes, but they freeze well. Alternatively you can make half quantity, using one small egg and very little milk.

Traditionally eaten cold, but they are hard to resist straight from the pan especially when children are about. They are never buttered.

Chris Williams
Teacher Class 5

SUGAR AND SPICE RINGS

½ lb self-raising flour
¼ level tsp salt
1½ oz English or Welsh butter
¼ pint milk

Filling:
1 oz English or Welsh butter, melted
2 oz castor sugar
1 level tsp cinnamon
1½ oz currants

Sift flour and salt into bowl. Rub in butter finely. Add milk all at once. Mix to soft, but not sticky, dough with a knife. Turn on to a lightly floured board. Knead quickly until smooth and then roll into rectangle approximately 8 inches x 12 inches. Brush with butter to within ¼ inch of edges. Mix sugar with cinnamon and currants, then sprinkle over butter.

Moisten edges of dough lightly with water. Roll up like a Swiss roll, starting from one of the longer sides. Cut into 12 slices. Arrange, cut sides down, in an 8 inch well-buttered round cake tin or fairly deep sandwich tin.

Bake towards top of hot oven (425°F/Gas Mark 7) for 15 to 20 minutes (or until well risen and golden). Turn out onto a wire cooling rack. Leave until lukewarm. Gently pull apart to separate rings. Serve as they are or with extra butter. Serves 4 to 6.

Jean Ross
Teacher, Class 1

CARAMEL SHORTCAKE

Shortbread:

12 oz self-raising flour
8 oz margarine
4 oz castor sugar

Line two Swiss roll tins with baking parchment. Rub the margarine into the flour until it resembles breadcrumbs. Add the sugar and combine the mixture into a smooth dough.

Divide the mixture between the two tins and press in firmly to cover the base of each tin. Bake at 160°C/300°F/Gas Mark 2 until golden brown.

Caramel:

Place the following ingredients, <u>except the chocolate</u>, into a saucepan:-

8 oz margarine
4 oz sugar
4 tbsp golden syrup
1 x 397 g tin sweetened condensed milk
Chocolate for the topping

Bring the first four ingredients slowly to the boil and cook gently for 5-10 minutes stirring constantly to prevent burning. Leave to cool for a few minutes, and then pour onto the cooled shortbread.

When the caramel has cooled, melt sufficient chocolate to cover the mixture. Cut into squares when the chocolate has set.

Janet Dennis
School Office Assistant

SPICED APPLE CAKE

75 g/3 oz Granny Smith apples, cored and diced
Squeeze of lemon juice
225 g/8 oz plain flour
1½ tsp baking powder
Pinch of salt
100 g/4 oz unsalted butter, cubed
75 g/3 oz sugar
25 g/1 oz sultanas
25 g/1 oz raisins
2 eggs, beaten
2 tbsp milk

Mix the apples in a bowl with the lemon juice and put aside.

Sift flour, baking powder, cinnamon and salt into a bowl and rub in butter to breadcrumb stage. Stir in sugar, walnuts, sultanas and raisins. Add the apples and lemon juice to the mixture and stir. Then add the eggs and enough milk to make a soft dough.

Pour the mixture into an 18cm/7in greased and lined deep, loose-bottomed cake tin. Tap tin on a worktop to remove bubbles and smooth the surface. Bake at Gas Mark 4/350°F/180°C for about an hour or until an inserted skewer comes out clean.

Cool the cake in the tin and then turn out onto a wire rack. Serve in slices. Serves 10.

Anne Hoskins
School Finance & Administration Officer

CHOCOLATE SLICE - to serve 50 people !

680 g flour
680 g margarine
680 g sugar
225 g coconut
110 g glacé cherries (chopped)
110 g cornflakes (crushed)
55 g cocoa
50 g baking powder
450 g chocolate topping

1. Crush the cornflakes.
2. Mix everything together.
3. Grease 2 big baking tins.
4. Divide mix into the 2 tins.
5. Cook in oven at 400°C for 20 minutes.
6. Cut whilst hot.
7. Then coat with chocolate.

Tracy, Cheryl and Natalie
Our School's Canteen Staff

TRAFFIC LIGHTS

6 oz milk chocolate
3 oz broken biscuits, roughly crushed
6 oz can condensed milk
Red, yellow and green glacé cherries

Melt the chocolate in a bowl over a pan of hot water and stir occasionally until quite smooth. Remove from the heat and stir in biscuits and milk.

Turn into a 7 inch greased square tin and smooth flat. Leave in refrigerator until set and then cut into 8 bars. Decorate each bar with halved cherries in the pattern of traffic lights.

Ronnie Stone
Chair of School Governors

MUM'S POTATO CAKES

2 lb potatoes   *Milk*
Butter   *Salt and pepper*
Self raising flour

Boil potatoes until soft, drain and mash in the usual way with butter, milk and seasoning. Add a little more butter so that the mixture is quite soft and creamy. Leave until almost cold, add the flour (about one to one and a half cupfuls or until the mixture resembles a stiffish dough). It is also rather sticky.

Take a portion of the mixture (about a sixth) and place on a well-floured board. Your hands will also need to have a lot of flour on them. Pat the mixture until flat and about three-quarters of an inch thick. You can use a rolling pin, being very careful that the mixture doesn't stick to either the board or the rolling pin.

Place the potato cakes on large baking tray and bake in a moderately hot oven for 15 to 20 minutes or until golden brown.

Eat straight away, spread with a little butter.

Phillip Schofield

FRENCH TOAST
A GOOD AFTER SCHOOL SNACK

4 eggs   *1 cup milk*
¼ cup sugar   *6-8 slices day old bread*

Mix eggs, milk and sugar together in a bowl large enough to take one slice of bread. Heat frying pan with knob of butter. Dip slices of bread one at a time into the mixture, and turn them over to coat both sides. Fry the slices until brown on both sides. Remove from pan and cool. Put each slice into a plastic bag to freeze.

When hungry, remove from freezer and pop under the grill. When hot, serve with your favourite sauce or jam.

Alan and Debbie Gilbert,
Ponderosa Restaurant, Redruth

GUINNESS CAKE

8 oz butter
8 oz dark brown sugar
2 large eggs
10 oz plain flour
1 tsp mixed spice

4 oz mixed peel
4 oz walnuts, coarsely chopped
8 oz sultanas
8 oz raisins

Guinness - 4 tbsp for mixing the cake and 8 tbsps to soak after cooking

Line a deep cake tin with greased brown paper. Set the oven at 150°C.

Cream butter and sugar. Add the eggs. Then fold in the sieved flour and mixed spice. Add the mixed peel, walnuts, sultanas and raisins and 4 tablespoons of Guinness.

Mix well, turn mixture into the prepared tin and bake for 1 – 1½ hours at 150°C, then another 1½ hours at 140°C. Test with skewer to make sure it is cooked, turn out onto a cooling rack.

When it is completely cooled, turn it upside down and prick the base all over with a skewer. Pour over the other 8 tablespoons of Guinness to soak in. Wrap the cake up in greaseproof paper and put the cake away for one week.

Teresa Mazzeo,
who did the fundraising for our book.

WEETABIX CAKE

2 Weetabix
8 oz soft brown sugar
8 oz combination of any mixed dried fruit, e.g. 2 oz sultanas,
        2 oz apricots, 2 oz raisins, 2 oz dates, etc
8 oz self-raising flour
1 egg
½ pint milk

Mix together the Weetabix, sugar and fruit. Add the milk and leave to soak overnight. Add egg and flour, and mix well. Pour into a lined loaf tin. Bake in oven 180°C for about 1¼ hours.

Daphne James
Our School's Lollipop Lady

CORNISH RECIPES

SAFFRON BUNS

1¾ lb plain flour
½ tsp salt
6 oz currants
6 oz sultanas
2 oz lard
2 oz margarine
4 oz castor sugar
1 oz fresh yeast
1 egg
¾ pint lukewarm milk
1 sachet saffron

Chop the saffron into small pieces with scissors and pour on a little boiling water. Leave it to soak overnight.

Mix the yeast with a little of the sugar and put to one side in a warm place. Meanwhile, rub the fat into the flour and stir in the fruit, salt and remaining sugar. Beat the egg and milk together, stir in the saffron and the yeast, which should now be starting to bubble. Gradually mix in the dry ingredients to make a firm dough. Cover with a cloth and put in a warm place to prove.

In an hour the mixture should double in size. Knead it and shape it into buns. Leave to stand on a greased oven proof baking tray for another half an hour, during which time the buns will double in size again.

Bake for 10-15 minutes at Gas Mark 5/425°F.

Adrian Roberts
School Governor

CORNISH PASTY

To make an 8 inch round of pastry

6 oz made pastry -
Half fat to flour, e.g. 1lb flour, ¼ lb butter and ¼ lb lard

1 oz sliced turnip or swede
2 oz sliced potato
4 oz finely chopped pin round or other good quality steak
1 tbsp finely chopped onion
Pepper and salt to taste

Roll out pastry and cut to size. Fold in half.

Open it out and layer up the vegetables and meat in this order from bottom up - turnip – potatoes – meat – onion – pepper and salt.

Moisten edge of pastry. Press edges together and crimp starting from the right hand side. Brush with beaten egg. Bake in hot oven 180-200°C for ¾ hour.

Marie Trevithick, Chairman
Redruth Ladies Lifeboat Guild

RUSSIAN CREAM

Despite its title, this is a traditional Cornish recipe.

1 pint milk
2 eggs
Gelatine (i.e. 1 packet gelatine made with ¼ cup water)
4 oz caster sugar

Separate egg whites and whisk until firm. Dissolve gelatine in hot water then mix with beaten yolks and sugar, stirring all the time. Warm milk to just below boiling point, add egg yolks, sugar and gelatine. Heat gently <u>without boiling</u>, then slowly stir this into the egg whites. Mix gently but thoroughly.

Put in dish(es) and leave to set. Decorate with chocolate flake or as desired.

Russell Grigg
President, Redruth Rotary Club

CORNISH HEAVY CAKE (HEAVA CAKE)

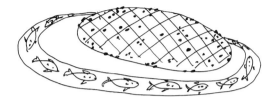

6 oz plain flour
3 oz fat – half lard and half margarine
1½ oz sugar
3 oz mixed fruit
Peel if liked
½ tsp salt

Mix flour, salt and fat roughly together. Add the other ingredients and mix well. Mix with water to stiff dough. Roll out to approximately half inch thick into an oval shape. Criss cross with a knife.

Bake at 350°F for 25-30 minutes

This was a cake that the fishermen's wives used to bake when they were expecting their husbands home from sea. They would go up to the cliffs, and when they saw shoals of fish near the boats they would signal by shouting "Heava, Heava!". Then they went home and made this quickly baked cake. It is shaped into an oval and criss crossed to represent the fishing nets.

Mrs Connie Richards, Chairperson
Guild of Friends of Camborne-Redruth
Community Hospital

THE CORNISH PASTY RECIPE WHICH WON
THE BBC 2 "FOOD AND DRINK" COMPETITION

Pastry –
I was once told to treat pastry like a best friend and bread dough like your worst enemy! So here goes.

For 4 – 6 pasties, 6 inch or 8 inch rounds. If you're a farmer, an 8-inch round is definitely for a hungry man.

12 oz strong plain flour
12 oz plain flour (cheapest will be fine)
1½ tsp salt
6 oz white fat
4 oz hard margarine
2 tsp vinegar

Mix the flours together with the salt. Rub fats into flour until a fine breadcrumb mixture is formed. Add 8-9 tablespoonfuls of very cold water mixed with the vinegar. It is essential that the mixture is on the wet side – a soft pliable dough. And I always roll each round separately – thus avoiding over rolling the pastry. Any scraps can be kneaded gently into the next round. The pastry should be about ¼ inch thick.

The inside story -
For each pasty
One medium potato and 1 slice of swede or turnip, chipped, cubed and thinly
*   sliced*
2-3 oz beef skirt cut small, beef chuck steak will do
2 slices onion (red onion doesn't repeat if finely chopped)
Seasoning: freshly ground black pepper and sea salt for preference
Thumb-nail size knob of butter
½ tsp flour for each pasty

Mix the ingredients into a bowl, apart from the seasoning, butter and flour.

NOTE if the pasties are to stand before cooking, the sliced potatoes should be well rinsed, then dried, before adding to the mixture. The water rinses away the starch, which would discolour the potatoes. (I use a salad spinner to extract the water from the potatoes.)

Put the filling onto the centre of the pastry rounds. Sprinkle with the seasonings, then flour and lastly put the knob of butter on the top. Draw up the edges of the pasty and pinch together. Begin at one end and fold pinch, fold pinch all the way across – 21 crimps, so I'm told.

Brush with beaten egg after placing on baking trays lined with bakewell paper. It is not necessary to poke, prod or pierce the pasties before cooking.

Cook 450°F/220°C/Gas Mark 8, or an Aga if you have one, for three quarters to one hour, or until the pasty will move freely on the bakewell paper and the underside of each pasty is golden brown and cooked through.

Then enjoy!

Jackie Martin

HELFORD OYSTERS

Half way through cooking a fillet of beef, stuff it with oysters. This is known as a "Carpet-Bagger Steak"!

Wrap oysters in bacon and grill them. This is called "Angels on Horseback".

But the only way to eat Native Oysters, in my opinion, is on the shell - raw and with a twist of lemon.

Lindsay Hodges, Manager
The Duchy of Cornwall Oyster Farm

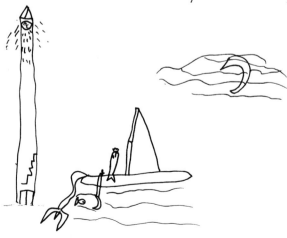

CORNISH FISH PIE

As some Cornish producers struggle to survive, it's good to be able to support them by using local vegetables and fish in this pie. I like to make this because you don't have to be too accurate with the ingredients – a bit extra fish or fewer potatoes won't make too much difference! It's good "comfort" food – just right for a cold and wet winter's evening – and we have quite enough of those!

1½ lb white or smoked fresh CORNISH fish
1 lb CORNISH potatoes
2 large CORNISH onions
You will also need a small amount of butter and a small piece of hard farmhouse cheese (both CORNISH of course!)
Butter, milk and flour for a white sauce

Sauté the chopped onion in the butter until soft and golden. Add the flaked cooked fish (I cook it in the microwave – is that cheating?) and turn it lightly into the onion in a pie dish. Try to do this without breaking up the fish too much. (If it's for a special occasion you could also add a handful of prawns.)

Make a basic white sauce – butter, flour and milk – season it well, and pour it over the fish and onions. I normally add a blob or two of mixed Dijon mustard just to spice things up a bit.

In the meantime steam and mash some potatoes (yes, I know, MORE washing up but it IS worth it!) and then fork them over the top of the fish/sauce mixture. Sprinkle some grated cheese over the top and bake it in a hot oven until golden brown and bubbling. It's great with some steamed CORNISH broccoli!

Tim Hubbard
BBC Radio Cornwall, Winner of the Sony Gold
1999 News Broadcaster of the Year Award

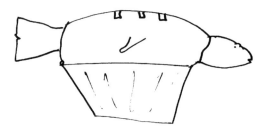

FARMHOUSE CLOTTED CREAM

4 – 6 pints of FRESH FULL CREAM MILK.
This will yield 4 – 6 ounces of clotted cream.

Preparation

Carefully pour the top quarter pint of cream from each pint of milk into a suitable shallow bowl or pan with a wide surface area. Allow the container to stand for 12 hours (or overnight) in a cool place.

Method

When a good cream line has been obtained, the container is placed on a source of heat for the scalding period. (NB <u>Avoid direct heating of the cream.</u>) Use a 'double pan' containing a water jacket.

Bring the water in the pan to the boil, then place the cream container into the pan. <u>Do not cover the cream</u>. Allow the cream to steam for approximately 35-45 minutes. When bubbles formed on the surface of the 'crust' have burst, the cream is usually ready to remove from the heat. Place the cream in a cool place and leave for 12 hours.

Finally, use a perforated utensil to skim off the clotted cream, ready for serving.

Eleanor Mundy
Recently retired teacher

A PROPER CORNISH CREAM TEA

Mrs Rodda's own recipe for Cornish Splits. Your favourite jam and a helping of genuine clotted cream, spread as generously as traditional Cornish hospitality, will give you the true taste of Cornwall. "A proper cream tea."

For the splits you will need the following ingredients:

1 lb strong white flour   *1 tsp salt*
¼ lb plain flour   *1 oz fresh yeast*
1 tsp sugar   *3 oz lard or margarine*
Just over ½ pint of warm milk

Mix the yeast and sugar until liquid and add to the warm milk. Sieve the flour and salt and rub in the fat. Add sufficient liquid to make workable dough. Knead well and allow to prove until double the size. Knead again and make into rolls or buns, and place on a floured baking sheet. Prove again in a warm place until double in size and bake at 350°C for twenty minutes.

Mrs Betty Rodda
Rodda's Creamery, Cornwall

CORNISH CRAB TART

8 oz shortcrust pastry, with a little mustard powder mixed in the dry ingredients
6 oz white crab meat
2 oz chopped parsley
½ pint single cream
2 egg yolks
Salt and pepper

Roll out the pastry and line an 8-inch flan ring or tin. Lightly prick the base of the flan with a fork.

Evenly distribute the crab on the pastry. Combine cream, egg yolks, parsley and seasoning and pour over crabmeat.

Cook on a baking sheet in a moderate oven for 40 minutes. Serves 4 – 6.

Vince Falco
Cornwall College, Camborne

TESENNOW PATATA KERNEWEK MAMWYN
(or a VAMWYN)

Defnythyow:
(½) hanter pos patatys bryjyes ha brewys
(3-4) try dhe beswar uns bles
(2) deu uns amanyn
holan

Forth:

Kemysk an patatys brewys godom gans amanyn ha holan hag ena gor ynno an bles. Kemysk yn tyen dhe gafos levender compes. War vord blesek po plat blesek gwra a'n kemyskyans tesennow cren ogas ha (2) dyw vesva yn musur a drus hag ogas ha (¾) try quartron mesva yn tewder. Gor y a denewan rak yeynhe yn tyen.

Gor blonek yn padel-frya ha poth hy yn tyen. Fry an tesennow bys pan yns-y cras ha gorm war aga deu du ha deber poth. – Pur whek hag ow-lenwel.

Y a yl bos dyghtyes gans kyk ha losow mes ow thylu a's car aga honen.

Ann Trevenen Jenkin,   Barth Mur

Translated from the Cornish recipe above –

GRANNIE'S CORNISH POTATO CAKES

½ lb boiled and mashed potatoes	*3-4 oz flour*
2 oz butter	*Salt*

Mix the warm mashed potatoes with butter and salt and then put in it the flour. Mix thoroughly to get an even smoothness. On a floured board or a floured plate make of the mixture round cakes about 2 inches in diameter and about three quarters of an inch thick. Put them aside to cool completely.

Put fat in a frying pan and heat thoroughly. Fry the cakes until they are crisp and brown on their two sides and eat hot. Delicious and filling.

They can be served with meat and vegetables but my family like them on their own.

Ann Trevenen Jenkin,   Grand Bard, Cornish Gorsedd

HELSTON PUDDING

2 oz raisins

2 oz currants

2 oz sugar

2 oz fresh breadcrumbs

2 oz flour

A pinch of salt

2 tbsp ground rice

2 tbsp grated suet

½ tsp mixed spice

½ tsp bicarbonate of soda

6 tbsp milk

1 tbsp finely chopped peel

Dissolve the bicarbonate of soda in the milk. Mix all the dry ingredients together thoroughly, and then add the milk and bicarbonate of soda mixture. Mix well again. Pour into a well-greased basin. Cover with greased paper with a tuck in it to allow for expansion. You can either boil or steam the pudding for 2 hours. Serves 4 – 6 people.

Helston Pudding is very good served with Lemon Sauce:

Boil 6 oz sugar with half a pint of water for five minutes. Remove from the heat and add 2 teaspoons of butter and 1 tablespoon of fresh lemon juice. When all the butter has melted into the sauce, stir well and pour over the top of the unmoulded pudding.

Tony Whitmarsh
Our School's Caretaker

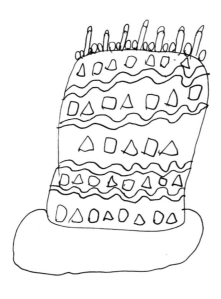

MISCELLANEOUS

ALPINE STRAWBERRY JAM

Save the fruits regularly by freezing them until the season is over. Collect all fruits except the mouldy ones, even half-ripe ones will make jam – but of course the ripest have the best flavour. Clean frozen berries of bulk of seeds by rubbing them on a clean towel before they defrost. Add half their own weight of apple juice, redcurrant juice or water with a little lemon juice in it. Simmer till softening completed, then add the same total weight of white cane sugar. Boil till setting point is reached then jar or bottle.

You can reduce the sugar content and the boiling time considerably, but you will need to keep the bottled jam in a fridge.

Sow the seeds removed earlier, as they may well germinate.

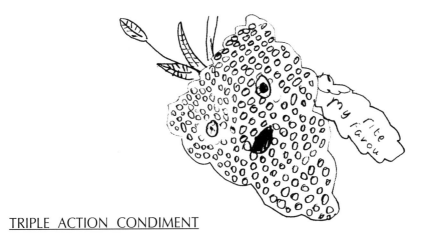

TRIPLE ACTION CONDIMENT

Mix one part pulverised garlic with one part pure ground yellow mustard and two parts pulverised horseradish. Stir to a paste with spirit vinegar. Leave to mature for three months in refrigerator and then use sparingly. Especially good toasted on top of cheese on toast.

Bob Flowerdew
Gardener Extraordinaire

LEMON ICE CREAM SODA

Try adding 2 tablespoons lemon juice in a nice tall glass with 2 tablespoons of sugar. Stir until dissolved. Add soda until the glass is two thirds full. Then top up with a large scoop of vanilla ice cream. Finally garnish with fruit.

The result is wonderful.

CARDINAL PUNCH

Try and get children to eat or drink anything that you simply say is good for them. However, it if looks good – that is a different matter. This recipe is wonderful on both counts. It's also easy to make in large quantities so it can be great for children's parties.

To a jug of ice add four parts of cranberry juice, two parts of lemon juice and top it up with ginger ale. Add an assortment of fresh fruit.

Not only does it taste great, but you can it eat it with a spoon – and that has the great effect of entertainment value for a good ten minutes!

BANANA FROTHY

Sitting on a hot summer's day in the garden searching for a refreshing drink, I remembered the pleasure of an ice-cold milk shake as a child.

It was simple. One pint of ice cold semi skimmed milk. 2 scoops of Cornish dairy ice cream, 6 ice cubes and one ripe banana.
A blitz in the liquidizer to ensure it was drinkable with a straw.

But the pleasure came from the drinking.

Aaron Pascoe
Penventon Hotel, Redruth

"IRISH CREAM LIQUEUR"

Note: this recipe contains uncooked eggs

3 fresh eggs
1 400 g tin condensed milk
2 tbsp Camp coffee
1 full cup whisky
1 carton long life double cream

Whip the long life double cream until thick, put aside. Whip the three fresh eggs until thick and frothy. Mix eggs and cream together, add condensed milk, coffee and whisky. Mix well together. Bottle and keep in fridge. When bottling the drink, leave enough room at the top to enable you to shake the bottle well, as the drink becomes thick.

Keep bottles in refrigerator and shake well before pouring out a drink. Make sure you finish drinking all your home-made Irish Cream Liqueur before the date marked on the long life double cream carton! Makes two bottles.

Melanie Giles
School Support Staff

NORWEGIAN PUMPKIN PICKLE

Pumpkins are fun and easy to grow, and are getting more and more popular in the British Isles. We'd like to share this pickle recipe, which was given to us many years ago by Norwegian friends. It tastes and looks like mango chutney, is a lovely golden colour with a thick consistency, and goes beautifully with Indian food, baked potatoes and cold meat. It keeps in good condition for years.

Prepare a pumpkin by cutting it into 'boat' shaped sections to make it easier to handle – anything from 14 to 16 depending on its size. By the way, if you are choosing pumpkins for cooking, whether it is pies, soups or pickles, go for the most solid you can find. The heavier they seem for their size, the denser and better flavoured and less watery the flesh will be.

Peel the boat sections, remove the seed and pith, and cut them into pieces roughly 1-inch square. Weigh them. Cover them with an inch of water and boil for about 5 minutes. Strain.

Make vinegar for pickling as follows:
For every 2 lbs of pumpkin allow ¾ pint of malt vinegar, 2lbs of sugar, 2-3 ozs of root ginger cut into roughly 1-inch lengths. (You can cut back on the sugar if you feel guilty about that quantity.) Boil for 5 minutes.

Add the pumpkin cubes to the vinegar mixture. Boil together until most of the liquid has evaporated. It can take up to an hour. Pack into screw top jars.

Joy Larkcom
Gardening Writer

ELDERFLOWER CORDIAL

This popular country recipe uses flowers from the Elder tree. This hardy deciduous shrub or tree grows abundantly in Cornwall to a height of 12 feet. The Elder's creamy white flowers bloom in the summer and produce a beautiful scent. The flowers can also be used in skin and hair preparations, and for vinegars, wines and cordials. The ripe berries can be used in jam making.

2 unwaxed lemons
200 g (7 oz) white sugar
600 ml (1 pt) water
6 heads of elderflowers, washed
2 tsp citric acid (sour salt)

Prepare bottles or jars by cleaning thoroughly, preferably sterilising.

Scrub and peel the lemons, reserving the peel. Cut the lemons in half, and squeeze and strain the juice. Put the sugar and water in a pan and bring to the boil. Add the elderflowers and simmer for 10 minutes. Add the lemon rind to the syrup and leave to infuse until cool.

Strain the syrup, then dissolve the citric acid in the lemon juice and add to the syrup. Pour into bottles and store in the refrigerator.

Dilute to taste with water, soda water, lemonade or your favourite mixer. This muscat-flavoured, lemony syrup can also be used with other drinks and cocktails.

Susan Ledingham
School Governor

Treloweth Primary School would like to thank all the following individuals and businesses for their financial support towards the printing costs of our book.

All Days	Pooley's Freezer Centre
ATS Tyres	Powell's Garage
Beez Neez Computers	R E & S Pearce
Brian Saunders, Chemist	Robert's Fish and Chips
Crystal Image	S J Bartle
Dennis & Stevens	Sacha, Viscountess Villiers
Dragon Spring	Sat-Tech TV Audio
Duchy Concrete	Second Spin
E Williams	Stop in Shop
Fast Lady Restaurant	Talking Heads
Grate Expectations	The Bassett Count House
Keast Newsagents	The Bond Street Optician
Knitcraft	The Cheese Board
La Belle	The Cornish Oven
Londis	The Noshery
MacSalvors Ltd	The Red Lion
Maynes Garage	The Wool Basket
Mr Chips	Vale's Fish and Chips
One & All Sports	W R Nicholas Chemist Ltd
Ponderosa Restaurant	Wool & Craft & Fabric
Pool Post Office	

THANK YOU